What Bible Can You Trust?

BROADMAN PRESS/Nashville, Tennessee

Library of Congress Catalog Card Number: 73-83828
Dewey Decimal Classification: 220.5
Printed in the United States of America

Contents

Preface

Because so few Christians can read the Bible in its original languages, translations are essential to Christian worship, Bible study, and devotional reading. One translation—the King James Version—has had the largest circulation and widest use for more than three centuries. During the last hundred years, however, new manuscript discoveries and drastic changes in the English language of everyday communication influenced a growing number of translations of the Bible.

As might be expected, the reaction to the diversity of translations has been varied. Students and other young people have been enthusiastic about the modern language versions. Their elders generally prefer the 1611 translation because of what it has meant to them in worship and in times of joy and stress. Some religious bodies seem to be dependent on the King James Version, while others encourage variety in Bible text for worship and study.

This book takes the middle ground, recognizing that the Bible is intended to be both understood and appreciated. It accepts the value of all translations which are honest efforts to help God's Word be meaningful to more people.

We invited the originators and/or publishers of ten modern translations to describe briefly the purpose and distinctives of their works. Each responded generously and honestly. We added brief descriptions of six other translations and introduced the whole of chapter 3 with a section on the King James Version. All seventeen statements are arranged chronologically according to publication date of each complete Bible, or of the New Testament if that is all that has been produced.

Pastors, Bible professors, editors, and other denominational leaders were asked to write briefly about which translations they use and why. Twenty-six responded from fifteen states and their statements are arranged alphabetically in chapter 4. Almost all of them read the King James Version in the pulpit but use three or more modern translations in their Bible study.

We are grateful to all these contributors and to Dr. Eugene A. Nida for permission to use as our chapter 2 a chapter from his book *God's Word in Man's Language*.

1. Why So Many Bibles?

Every year or so—at least, so it seems—a new English translation of the Bible is announced. The visitor to a well-stocked religious book store is confronted with an array of ten to twenty different versions. In the face of this abundance, there is little wonder that many Christians are puzzled. If so many versions are needed, are all reliable? If some are not reliable, which ones are? Is there a Bible translation that you can trust?

The flood of English translations goes back more than five hundred years. In less than a hundred years before the publication of the King James Version in 1611, at least eight major English versions appeared. During the next two hundred years over twenty new translations were made. But the greatest outpouring has come in the twentieth century. This book seeks to help you understand why so many translations have been made and how you may select one or more for your own use. It introduces ten translations that enjoy wide use today, and it shares the views of pastors and other Christian leaders about what translations they prefer and why.

The Long Shadow of the Past

The medieval church did not favor Bible reading by lay people, and it sought to suppress the translation of the Bible into English. There was, however, one major translation during this period—that of John Wycliffe. Printing had not yet been invented in Europe, and so copies of Wycliffe's Bible were made by hand and circulated at great cost—as well as at risk of life.

The first printed English Bible was a translation by William Tyndale, which appeared in sections between 1525 and Tyndale's martyrdom in 1536. Enemies of Bible translation managed to take Tyndale's life, but they did not stop his influence. His work is reflected in most subsequent translations, including the famous King James Version. Other influential versions of this early period include the Bishops' Bible, prepared for use in the Church of England, and the Geneva Bible, translated by English Puritans. These two versions eventually were replaced by the King James Version, but not for about fifty years after 1611.

King James I followed Elizabeth I on the throne of England. He was interested in religion and was a strong advocate of the Church of England. In fact, he allowed no religious freedom for anyone who did not accept the Church of England system, with its strong control by bishops under the rule of the king. James showed his sentiments in 1612 by imprisoning Thomas Helwys, pioneer English Baptist, who contended that the king did not have the right to dictate religious beliefs for his subjects.

Shortly after he came to the throne, James organized a committee of Church of England scholars to make a new Bible translation. When it was published in 1611, advocates of earlier translations, such as the Bishops' Bible and the Geneva Bible, did not favor it. In the course of about fifty years, however, it won acceptance as the standard English translation. New translations were made in the following centuries, but it was not until 1870 that a movement was launched which seriously challenged its place.

The Demand for Change

The same Church of England that produced the King James Version started the movement a century ago to replace it. This time, however, its leaders were more tolerant of other Christians. Plans were begun in 1870 that resulted in publication of the English Revised Version in 1881-1885. Not only Church of England (Episcopal) but Baptist, Methodist, Congregational, and Presbyterian scholars helped to produce the new translation.

Since the King James Version was so widely used and loved, why was change considered necessary? Two significant reasons were the changes in the English language that had taken place since 1611 and the discovery of important texts of the Greek New Testament.

English always has been a language "on the move." It not only adds new words all of the time but even changes the meanings of old ones. A famous example in Bible translation is "prevent" as used in the King James Version in 1 Thessalonians 4:15. The meaning here is "precede" or "go before." "Prevent," however, has totally lost this meaning, making the King James translation of the verse unintelligible.

The matter of Greek texts is not so obvious but equally demanding from the view of Bible scholars. The King James Version was based on a few Greek manuscripts of the New Testament. In the centuries that followed, other manuscripts were discovered. Careful study during the nineteenth century revealed that many of the recent discoveries were actually older and more reliable copies of the original writings.

Early scribes who copied the New Testament manuscripts usually tried to be accurate, but mistakes occurred. On top of this, a few deliberate changes were made—little additions that sought to explain or clarify, or even longer ones that seemed appropriate at the time.

Uncovering the older manuscripts during the nineteenth century indicated that many minor changes and a few major ones had corrupted the manuscripts used by the King James translators. For example, Matthew 6:13 in the King James Version concludes Jesus' prayer with the familiar and well-loved words: "For thine is the kingdom, and the power, and the glory, for ever. Amen." These words seem to "belong" to the prayer, but they are not in the most reliable manuscripts. Other longer additions include Mark 16:9-20, John 5:4, and John 7:53 to 8:11. New translations indicate, by one device or another, that these passages appear to have been added to the original New Testament writings. Scanning the footnotes in a modern translation will show that there are scores of shorter additions of this type.

To deal with such problems, the English Revised Version was published in 1881-1885. This was followed in 1901 by the American Standard Version, based on the English work but including a number of changes favored by the American translators.

These two versions aimed for accuracy in translation and faithfulness to the best Greek texts. They retained, however, much of the old style of phrasing which marks the King James Version. They broke ground by calling attention to the need for new translations, but they did not fully meet that need.

The Language of the People

The New Testament was written in Greek, but it is Greek that differs in many ways from the classics of Greek literature. Students of the Greek language long ago noticed the difference, but they did not know what it meant. Bible students came to assume that the New Testament was written in a special sacred language. Then, around the beginning of the twentieth century, a number of Greek documents were discovered in Egypt. These were everyday materials—letters, business contracts, and the like. They were written in the same period as the New Testament, and—to the astonishment of Greek scholars—they were written in the same language as the New Testament. The New Testament language was not some mysterious, special religious language but the everyday language of the first century! The only reason that this had not been recognized before was the fact that everyday writings from the period had never been studied carefully before. This form of Greek is now known as "koine" (koy-NAY), from the Greek word meaning "common" or "familiar."

These discoveries not only gave new understanding of the nature of New Testament language but actually added valuable information about the meanings of words. The twentieth century was faced with the requirement for an entirely new kind of Bible translation, one that would reflect the real character of Bible language. The result was the production of numerous modern-speech translations, such as those of James Moffatt and Edgar Goodspeed. For, as these men saw, only everyday English could truly present the everyday quality of New Testament Greek. The fancy, impressive phrasing of the King James Version, as beautiful as it sounds, misses the spirit of writings in the style and urgency of news dispatches.

Early modern-speech translations were the work of individual scholars. Dissatisfaction with the English and American revised versions called attention to the need for a new version to be prepared under church sponsorship. The International Council of Religious Education, an American interdenominational group, decided in 1929 to undertake such a new translation. This body developed the widely used International Sunday School lesson outlines for church use. It sought a new translation which would contribute to its role in church Bible teaching. Due to the financial depression of the 1930's, actual work on a new version was not begun until 1937. The Revised Standard Version of the New Testament was published in 1946. The Old Testament followed in 1952. This version sought to combine (1) the accuracy of translation of the English and American revised versions (1881 and 1901), (2) the literary beauty of the King James Version, and (3) the style or idiom of contemporary English speech.

The Revised Standard Version was more conservative than earlier twentieth-century translations in that it followed the King James Version and sought to make changes only when necessary. It was designed for use in public worship as well as private and class study. It was the work of outstanding American Bible scholars, and a large number of scholars were satisfied that it achieved its major objectives as a reliable and balanced contemporary translation.

Work on another major church-sponsored translation was begun in Great Britain in 1946. This resulted in publication of the *New English Bible*—the New Testament in 1961 and the Old in 1970. The introduction to the New Testament states: "The Joint Committee which promoted and controlled the enterprise decided at the outset that what was now needed was not another revision of the Authorized Version but a genuinely new translation, in which an attempt should be made consistently to use the idiom of contemporary English to convey the meaning of the Greek." This version, then, shares two of the three objectives of the Revised Standard— accurate translation and contemporary language. It differs sharply in that it makes no effort to retain the literary heritage of the King James (so-called Authorized) Version. It is essentially, therefore, a modern-speech translation. It differs from other modern-speech translations in being the work of a church-sponsored group of scholars. Americans also notice that it is marked by some British vocabulary that is unfamiliar to many American readers.

Many Private Translations

With the publication of the *New English Bible,* the number of church-sponsored translations comes to five: the King James, the English Revised, the American Standard, the Revised Standard, and the New English. The first enjoys more than three and a half centuries of use and an impressiveness of literary phrasing unmatched by any subsequent version. The second and third were significant as groundbreakers for a new era of translation— improvements over the King James for accuracy but often clumsy in phrasing. The fourth and fifth represent, in many ways, the best efforts of which English-speaking Bible scholarship is capable—accuracy in translation and phrasing vastly improved over the English and American revisions of 1881-1901. Yet the output of new translations continues. Some of these are individual efforts. Others are prepared by groups variously constituted. Why are potential translators encouraged to produce new efforts?

One reason is the impossibility of a perfect translation. Human language is ambiguous. To see this concretely, it is necessary only to look at a standard English dictionary. Most words have at least two or three definitions, some many more. That this is an inherent characteristic of language can be seen from looking at foreign-language dictionaries. Hebrew and Greek, the principal languages of the Bible, show the same fact. Hence the translator has a double problem—identifying the meaning in the original language and deciding how it best can be expressed in English.

It is not possible for even the most dedicated and competent Bible scholars to reach complete agreement on the original meaning. Even if final agreement about original meaning were possible, final expression in English would not be. Our language is too fluid. For example, when the Revised Standard New Testament was published in 1946, it seemed natural to retain the archaic pronouns "thou," "thy," and "thee" in prayer. The translators defended this as showing reverence. The Greek, of course, makes no comparable distinction. In the years since 1946 more and more Christians find it natural to address God in prayer as "you." This practice, at least, is more desirable than the curious mixture of "thou" and "you" that some Christians use in praying. Hence newer translations that completely avoid the "thou" forms now seem natural and adequately reverent.

A further problem is differing theological presuppositions on the part of translators. The translators selected to prepare the Revised Standard and New English versions had high academic standing and recognition within their respective denominations. Some Christians believe, however, that denominational leadership should not be fully trusted and that translators without strong denominational standing are more reliable.

Here we are in an area where feelings are strong and proofs are impossible. There simply is no way to establish that one set of translators is, for example, more committed in its Christian faith than another. Yet assumptions of this kind lie behind some translations that are in print.

Translations Under Attack

At least three translations have been subjected to attack by some who have questioned the theological stance of the translators involved. The Revised Standard New Testament was published in 1946 with a generally favorable reception. Shortly after publication of the Old Testament in 1952, however, the translation was strongly criticized by some Christians who felt that the translators were not theologically orthodox. This charge is no longer being widely made, but many Christians likely remember it. No major inaccuracy can be identified in the Revised Standard Version, but the fact that it was attacked causes some to question its reliability.

Less publicized but definite attacks have been made on *Today's English Version*, published by the American Bible Society, and *The Living Bible*, a paraphrase by Kenneth Taylor.

The Bible Society translation is based on a simple English vocabulary. It thus sometimes uses a familiar word in place of a more precisely literal word. This has upset some readers who feel that doctrinal care has been lost. It is well to remember that the New Testament originally was written in simple language.

The Living Bible has received very wide distribution in recent years and is appreciated by many Christian readers for its clear and fresh phrasing. Yet the translator has made clear from the outset that he was not attempting a precise translation but a paraphrase—a rephrasing to express the sense but not the exact wording. Criticism has come largely from Bible scholars who disagree with the translator about the meaning of certain passages. One has stated his opinion bluntly: "This is possibly the worst rendering of the Bible ever made into English." While such a statement may be extreme, it is a warning that a paraphrase does not possess the accuracy of a more careful translation.

One example of the kind of liberty that *The Living Bible* takes with the Bible text can be seen in John 19:26-27. These verses tell that Jesus entrusted the care of his mother to the disciple that he loved. This disciple, of course, is usually identified as John, and according to Christian tradition, John also wrote the Gospel that bears his name. *The Living Bible* thus substitutes "me" twice and "I" once for "the disciple."

The translator is assuming, as many Christians believe, that the disciple in question was in fact the writer of the Gospel. Yet this kind of translation is not true to the text. The translator is taking liberties that are not taken in the church-sponsored versions, the Revised Standard and the New English. In addition to the fact that the method is questionable, there is a more specific problem with this particular translation. John 19:35 and 21:24 indicate that the beloved disciple is the source of the information contained in the Gospel, but they appear to imply that he was not the actual writer.

What Bible Can You Trust?

The basic question raised by this book cannot be answered fully in this introductory chapter. The introductions to ten major translations in chapter 3 provide necessary details that cannot be summarized here. The comments by pastors and other Christian leaders in chapter 4 serve to illustrate why the writers make the choices that they do. Yet, in the end, the choice is left to you. The information that follows should help you make a choice, but it does not specify any one translation as the right choice for every Christian.

The following concepts may be of help as you consider the information that later sections present:

1. There is no single perfect translation. Each one has its strengths and weaknesses.

2. There is no seriously unreliable translation, in the honest judgment of the publisher, included among those that are described in following pages. Details can be questioned about every translation, but no one has shown any misleading statement of basic Christian truth in the translations under consideration.

3. Many Christians will continue to read and love the King James

Version, but at least one twentieth-century translation should be used along with it.

4. The two major translations sponsored by the Christian denominations, the Revised Standard and the New English, deserve special consideration. There is reason to believe that the kind of careful committee work underlying these works commends them above the work of individuals or other less representative groups.

5. Individual preference is a legitimate consideration. By reading representative sections of various translations, you can see which one or ones best speak to you the Word of God. Get the facts about the different translations, but let your choice be influenced by your own reading and response as well as the kind of information presented here.

2. From Hebrew and Greek into English

(This chapter appeared in *God's Word in Man's Language* (Harper and Brothers. 1952) by Eugene A. Nida under the title "Greek and Hebrew Treasures" and is being used by permission of the author.)

A carefully written letter from a devout lover of the Bible was received at the Bible House. In substance it read:

> I would be so glad to help in the translating of the Bible, and so if you would send me a dictionary and a grammar of some of these primitive languages, I would be happy to dedicate my spare time to the translation of the New Testament.

The desire to be of service to those who do not have the Bible is commendable, but no translator can obtain meaningful results by simply following intricately devised grammatical rules and matching words from the average dictionary. The true Bible translator must be a profound student of the native language, with all its rich cultural implications, and of the biblical languages, which he needs to study thoroughly in order to understand their historical setting.

No superficial knowledge of the Bible will suffice for the translator. Without thorough training he may discover that he is only passing on his own ignorance, based upon erroneous interpretations of words. How many people there are who think that "taking the Lord's name in vain" refers to common profanity! Perhaps in a sense it does, but the meaning of the Old Testament is not that the Lord's name is unmentionable in oaths, but that one should not swear by the Lord and then fail to perform one's promise. "Foreswearing" is not cursing, but promising to do something in the Lord's name and then failing to make good. The habit of using God's name had become so common and meaningless among the Jews that Jesus warned people not to use God's name at all, for they were making a mockery of their faith.

Some expressions in the Bible seem so perfectly obvious to us that we do not take the time to examine them or to inform ourselves more fully as to their possible meaning. When we read about "Simon the Cananaean" (Revised Standard Version), we take it for granted that "Cananaean" refers to the land from which he came. A close examination of this text in the Greek shows us that it is not the land at all. The word is a transliterated Aramaic term which means "zealot," that is, one who belonged to the rabid nationalist party. Knowing this, we can understand more easily why this same man is called "Simon Zelotes" in Acts 1:13 and "Simon the Cananaean" in Matthew 10:4. In Acts we have the Greek translation and in Matthew the Aramaic word borrowed into Greek. A man like Simon, so well known for his strong anti-Rome politics, would seem to some to be a liability for Jesus' political future. On the other hand, Jesus chose Levi, a publican, who had been regarded as a traitor to his own people by signing up with Rome to collect taxes for them. Within the small group of Jesus' own disciples there were these two men who represented opposite poles of political feeling and action. Neither of these men would be likely to enhance Jesus' political prestige, but he was obviously not courting earthly power but proclaiming the kingdom of heaven.

There are those who read into the Scriptures a justification for political haranguing of the multitudes. They argue, "But did not Jesus instruct us to 'preach upon the housetops' (Matt. 10:27)? Does not this imply shouting to the passing crowds in the streets below?" It would be so in our society, but the words of Jesus were addressed to the people of his day. What he meant was that his disciples should take what they heard from him in secret and should speak to their neighbors about it, as in the cool of the evening the families of the close-fitting houses gathered on near-by flat housetops to rest and chat. Jesus was not thinking of a political gathering, but of one neighbor telling another, witnessing of the faith that had become an intimate part of his life and something which he wished to share with his closest neighbor.

Some misinterpretations of the Bible result from changes in the meanings of words. In 1 Thessalonians 4:15 the words "we which are alive and remain . . . shall not prevent them which are asleep" seem to imply some peculiar doctrine of interference until we realize that this use of the word "prevent" is a very old one, reflecting its meaning in its original Latin value, namely, "to come ahead of." Such a verse should be translated as "shall not precede them which are asleep." In 2 Thessalonians 2:7 we encounter the strange rendering, "he who now letteth will let, until he be taken out of the way." This verse contains an old English word, which is only preserved in the legal phrase "let or hindrance" and in the tennis expression "a let ball." However, for most people the common usage is "net ball," not "let ball." This old word "let" meant "to hinder" or "to restrain." Hence a "let ball" is a hindered ball in tennis, but since it is usually hindered by the net, we generally speak about a "net ball." But in 2 Thessalonians 2:7 the meaning is that the One who now hinders or restrains shall continue to do so until He is taken out of the world.

Some mistranslations of the King James Version resulted from inadequate knowledge of the originals. This does not mean that the scholars who prepared the King James Version were not fully abreast of the biblical knowledge of their day. It only means that during the succeeding centuries we have been privileged to learn much more about the meanings of words and the significance of certain grammatical forms. In John 20:17 the King James reads "Touch me not," but the more correct translations read "Do not hold me" or even "Do not keep holding onto me." It was formerly thought that the different tenses of the Greek verb refer only to time, but we know now that they often signify different aspects or kinds of action. In this verse the Greek has a present form, which means that one is to cease doing what he is doing. If the verb had been an aorist, a different grammatical form of the verb, it would have meant not to do something in the future, that is, something not being done at the time. Not knowing about this subtle distinction, the translators of the King James did the best they could, but their translation has resulted in many rather fanciful explanations of how Jesus could not be touched because he had not presented himself in heaven, but how he did so in just a few minutes of time, since in Matthew 28:9 we read of Jesus meeting the women on their return to Jerusalem, and there the text says specifically that they touched his feet.

Many subtle distinctions in the original languages are difficult to translate in every instance, but whenever possible they should be properly treated. In Matthew 6 one encounters two forms of the verb meaning "to worry, to be anxious" (in the King James "take thought for"). In Matthew 6:25 the form of the verb means "do not continue to worry about." This is the present form of the verb, similar to the form occurring in John 20:17, noted just above. After Jesus has given his encouraging discourse on God's provision for the needs of his children, he then ends with a different form of the verb. In Matthew 6:34 the verb means "now don't worry any more about these things in the future." He begins his message by urging his followers to stop worrying and ends by assuming that they have ceased to worry and hence admonishes them never to worry again. In English translations it is awkward to convey all of this meaning without cumbersome phrases which tend to overtranslate the original, but in many other languages one can perfectly match certain of these intensely meaningful distinctions of the Greek.

There are some passages in the Scriptures in which the King James Version seems to suggest distinctions which are not to be found in the original. In Mark 1:4 one reads of the "remission of sins." For certain people the word "remission" has been regarded as a technical theological term, indicative of something rather different from "forgiveness." But in the Greek the word translated here as "remission" is just the common word "forgiveness." Accordingly, most of the more recent translations into English use the familiar and more meaningful term "forgiveness."

A close study of more modern translations and the careful reading of scholarly commentaries will help the Bible translator avoid many of the mistakes which would otherwise arise because of his limited understanding based on the traditional renderings. But there is really no substitute for at least some knowledge of the original languages. This knowledge must not be superficial or based upon apparent, but unreliable, etymologies or associations between words. Some people have argued that the Greek word *katabolê* could not possibly mean "foundation" or "establishment" (John 17:24 and Eph. 1:4) since its constituent parts mean "down" *(kata-)* and "to throw" *(bol-)*. They have insisted that such a word would have to mean "destruction." Hence they argue that "since the foundation of the world" in John 17:24 and elsewhere should be rendered as "since the destruction of the world." The reasons for this interpretation lie in certain fanciful ideas about various pre-Adamic dispensations, but from the standpoint of the Greek there is simply no justification for the meaning of "destruction." The meanings of words cannot be determined by pulling apart their components. If that were so, we would be hopelessly lost in attempting to explain the difference in meaning between the English nouns *up-set* and *set-up,* both having the same constituent parts, but meaning something quite different.

Some would-be students of Greek have insisted that the adjective *aiônios* must mean only "of an age" or "for an age" because it is related to the noun *aiôn* "age." But here again, the meaning is not determined by the similarities which a foreigner can discover between words, but by the manner in which these words are used by native speakers of the language. In John 3:16 the Scriptures are not speaking about "life for an age" but "eternal life." The student of the Bible must not dictate the meaning of the original words, but discover their meaning from their biblical contexts and from their wide use in non-biblical sources. Only by this means would he ever be able to recognize the fact that the Greek word *charis* can mean "beauty," "kindness," "grace," "gift," and "thankfulness." Similarly, the student of Hebrew finds the same root *nbl* in words meaning "shriveled," "wasted away," "crumbled to dust," "foolish," "impious," "carcass," "corpse," and "idol."

As anyone studies foreign languages there are many tempting etymologies which may suggest truths, but which may not be historically valid. This is true of some popular treatments of the Greek word *ekklêsia* "church." It is quite true that the Greek word comes from two roots which mean literally "called out." Many preachers have made use of this fact to point out helpful spiritual implications, and yet by New Testament times the word carried no such denotation as "called out." It was simply the word for "assembly" or "congregation." It so happened that in the Greek city-states an assembly of the citizenry resulted from the people being called out of their city and summoned from their farms to participate in such gatherings. Even though the etymology of the word remains, its real meaning is just "assembly," and a Greek-speaking person of New Testament times would be no more inclined to understand *ekklêsia* in its original etymological value of "called out" than we today would recognize "God be with you" in "goodby," which, as we may learn from the dictionary, was derived from the longer phrase.

We must not think, however, that because there are dangers in the misunderstanding of words, we should abandon the idea of probing the depths of lexical lore in order to understand and appreciate the Scriptures more fully. Nothing could be more untrue. The translator's work is immeasurably enriched by sound examination of the original languages. In fact, he must constantly make reference to the original languages since in direct proportion as he separates himself from the Greek and Hebrew by intervening languages, by the same degree does he tend to depart from the original meaning and lose the richness of the divine revelation.

Just a few Greek and Hebrew words will indicate something of the treasures which are in store for the one who will only go in search for them.

In Greek there are two words which are translated as "covenant," "contract," or "agreement." These are *diathêkê* and *synthêkê*, but only the first of these occurs in the New Testament. What, then, seems to be the reason why the Scripture writers employed only *diathêkê?* Is there some subtle distinction which we miss in English? There is. Both of these words may be used to denote a "covenant" or "contract," but by the use of *diathêkê* we understand that one person alone initiates the agreement and draws up the terms. It remains for others to accept or reject. It is for this reason that *diathêkê* is used to mean a "will" or "testament" since the one who wills his property is the one who takes the initiative in deter-. mining the contract, and he is the one who stipulates the conditions and rewards. In working out a *synthêkê* there are possibilities for arguments, concessions, compromise, and final bargaining by both parties, but in a *diathêkê* only one party to the covenant is respon- sible for its form. In this distinction lies one of the most profound truths of Scriptures. God is no one to be bargained with, for he will not settle for anything less than the best for man. In non-Chris- tian religions man is often regarded as a shrewd merchant with a record-keeping god or spirit. Man is thought to be able to pit his cleverness against the inattention of a deity in order to procure supernatural benefits at bargain rates. But there is no such basis for dickering with the God of Scripture. It is he who has established the covenant. We are the heirs. We can deny our sonship and waste our inheritance in riotous living, but God's plan will not be cheapened or his sovereignty infringed by clever men who refuse to accept the covenant of grace, established in the counsel of God and ratified by the death of his Son, for his was the blood of the new covenant (*diathêkê*, 1 Cor. 11:26).

The two most famous synonyms in Greek are *agapaô* and *phileô*, words which are both translated "love," and yet they denote quite different phases of this most powerful of all emotions. It has been said that *agapaô* refers to "the love of God" and *phileô* is only "the love of men." But this distinction is only a very small part of the difference, and as such is in itself incorrect. Both of these words may convey intense emotion or may be relatively weak in their meanings. These words do not indicate degrees of love, but kinds of love. *Agapaô* refers to love which arises from a keen sense of the value and worth in the object of our love, and *phileô* describes the emotional attachment which results from intimate and prolonged association. That is why in the Scriptures we are never commanded to "love" with the word *phileô*. Even when husbands and wives are instructed to love one another, the word *agapaô* is used, for it is impossible to command that kind of love which can arise only from intimate association. On the other hand, the saints are admonished to appreciate profoundly the worth and value in others, and *agapaô* is used to convey this meaning. All Christians are not necessarily to have sentimental attachments for one another *(phileô)*. This would be impossible, for our circle of intimate friends is limited by the nature of our lives. But we can all be commanded to appreciate intensely the worth of others. When "God so loved the world" (John 3:16) it was not with any sentimental attachment which he might have had for sinful mankind, but he looked upon men with the eyes of grace. He saw in men the worth which they had as his children, even when they persisted in their sinful rebellion. This was the redemptive love of *agapaô*.

The meaning of one difficult passage hinges primarily upon the meaning of one Greek word. When we read "A good tree bringeth not forth corrupt fruit, neither doth a corrupt tree bring forth good fruit" (Luke 6:43), we are puzzled at first, for we know quite well that many an old, rotten peach tree has still produced some delicious peaches and some very fine-looking trees produce very poor fruit, some of which may spoil while still on the tree. What then can be the meaning of this word "corrupt" (Greek *sapros*)? One clue is to be found in the use of this same word in the parable of the fishes which were taken in the great net (Matt. 13:47, 48). The good fish were put into vessels, but the bad fish (the Greek adjective *sapros* is used) were thrown away. Certainly, this net did not draw in rotting fish, but rather inedible fish. This word *sapros* designates inedible varieties. Now we may apply the word to the trees and the fruit. Some seedling trees, despite their beautiful appearance, produce inedible fruit. It is the very nature of the tree, and such a tree could not produce good fruit if it wanted to. In contrast, the tree which naturally produces edible fruit cannot produce the bitter inedible fruit, which is characteristic of some unbudded fruit trees. The proper understanding of this word *sapros* "corrupt" makes the entire parable take on new meaning. Men produce fruit in accordance with their basic nature. The outward appearance is unimportant; only the fundamental character counts. Hence, to produce the fruit of the Spirit, we must be ingrafted with the life of the Spirit of God. We must have a new nature. As Jesus expressed this truth to Nicodemus, we must be born anew.

Some words become encrusted with our own linguistic tradition, and only by returning to the Greek and Hebrew can we recapture the fundamental significance of the message of God's revelation. One group of such words comprises "saint," "holy," "sanctify," and "sanctification." With only an understanding of the connotations of these words in English we gather the impression that the Bible is talking about a kind of sanctimonious do-nothing religion, a twiddling of the thumbs in some pious atmosphere, the innocuous mumbling of well-memorized prayers, or the uninspired repetition of standard clichés which gain one the reputation of being spiritually minded, even though the heart may be wholly occupied with things of this world. Whatever positive significance we discover in these words is related simply to moral goodness, and reflects little of the holy grandeur which surrounds them in Hebrew and Greek. The Hebrew root *qdsh* and the Greek root *hag-* are not just synonyms for "good." Their primary significance is "set apart, consecrated, dedicated to the exclusive service of God." For us who have endeavored to defend the Christian religion in a humanistic society by emphasizing its ethical values, it comes as somewhat of a shock to find that one of the most crucial words in all the Scriptures is not primarily one of ethical content at all. It means "exclusive dedication to God." This truth becomes immediately apparent when we realize that the same Hebrew root is used in the words meaning "harlot" and "Sodomite." What were these poor creatures in pagan Semitic religion? They were devotees, consecrated to the sensual worship of their pagan deities. It is the old story of temple girls and boys, a practice still existing in some parts of the Orient, where people are dedicated to the gods for the purposes of sexual prostitution.

Where, then, did the Hebrew and Greek terms acquire the moral content which is reflected in our understanding of the corresponding words in English? The moral content comes from the nature of God and from the life which his worshipers are expected to live because they are consecrated to him. We need to capture again the consciousness of that awesome holiness, which characterizes the majesty of God. This will save us from the "chummy sentimentality" which is so common in some people's talk about the Eternal and will exalt our concept of consecration, for our holiness must reflect his holiness or it is not true holiness, only self-imposed piety.

It is easy to misinterpret the Old Testament because we may have too restricted an idea of the meanings of the words. The Hebrew term *nephesh,* frequently translated as "soul," has several meanings, including "breath," "life," "mind," "living thing," "animal," "person," and "self" (in such a phrase as "I myself"). In Ezekiel 18:4 people have tried to read into the statement, "The soul that sinneth, it shall die," some implications that would seem to refer to the destruction of the soul itself. But the entire context and the meaning of this word *nephesh* is quite contradictory to any such interpretation. What Ezekiel meant was, "The person who commits sin—and no one else—shall be punished for it."

There are some words which cannot be explained by all the detailed comments of exhaustive dictionaries. One such word is the Hebrew term *hesed*, translated variously as "mercy," "pity," "kindness," "love," "loving-kindness," "goodness," "compassion," "steadfast love," and "grace." But these words only begin to point out the rich connotation of this Semitic term. It is the steadfast love of a king for his subjects and the heartfelt devotion of subjects for their king; the intense kindness of God for his people, and the loyal love of the people for their God. Some translators have rendered it as "covenant love," but this is too restrictive. It is all-pervading emotion which binds God and man together and expresses itself in constant acts of mercy, kindness, and piety. Even then our best descriptions fall short of the full meaning of this word. We can only come to sense its significance as we read and reread the Law and the Prophets and there see how *hesed* describes the richness of mercy, love, and kindness which links God and man.

The translator who goes about his task faithfully and in so far as possible attempts to reckon with the biblical context, taking into consideration all the historical background for the revelation of God's Word, will discover not only rich meanings in the striking passages of great theological import, but he will also find some of the greatest proofs of the Bible's authenticity in those little words and phrases which one passes by almost without noticing. In Mark 1:32 we might feel that the writer was unduly repetitious when he says, "when evening had come and the sun had set." Why two phrases when one would seem to be sufficient? But in that repeated and emphasized phrase we have the key to the picture of what happened that day. Jesus had gone into the synagogue of Capernaum to teach. A man with an unclean spirit had come in and had cried out in recognition of Jesus of Nazareth. Jesus commanded the spirit to come out of the man and he was healed, much to the amazement of the crowd. After the service in the synagogue Jesus went with some of his disciples to Peter's home, but it was not until that evening when the sun had set and hence the Sabbath day had passed that these conscientious observers of the Jewish law dared to bring to him "all who were sick or possessed with demons." The fact that Jesus had healed a man on the Sabbath was not enough evidence that others should violate Sabbath regulations by seeking healing. One can picture these people waiting anxiously in their homes until finally the evening had come. Just as soon as the sun had set, they made all haste to bring to Jesus their sick and demon-possessed relatives and friends.

In Matthew 5:15 we are likely to accuse Jesus of hyperbole when he declares that men do not put a lamp under a bushel "but on a stand, and it gives light to all in the house." Knowing the kinds of small feeble lamps used in ancient times in the Jewish households it seems strange that he should have said, "to all in the house." "What about the other rooms of the house?" someone is likely to inquire. The truth of the matter is that Jesus was addressing himself to the common people, most of whom lived in one-room houses. Certainly, few of them could afford the luxury of several oil lamps. Jesus was talking to men and women in words and phrases which reflected their very lives.

To most of us the number of "a hundred and fifty-three," which was the number of fish caught in the net along the shores of Galilee after the resurrection (John 21:4-14), seems incredibly trifling. We might be inclined to wonder why the writer had any interest in giving the number. When, however, we realize that in ancient times the number 153 was given as the total number of all the tribes and nations of earth, it is no wonder that the early church interpreted this passage as the assurance of success in fulfilling the great commission to bear the Good News to all men everywhere.

Words do not always carry the same meanings in one language as they do in another. How strange it seems to us that Jesus would address his own mother as "woman" after her request at the wedding in Cana of Galilee and again from the cross. Such a term seems to indicate severity in Jesus' own nature and appears to imply some reproof for the mother who had been so faithful to him. This is because we do not realize that in the Greek of New Testament times the use of the word *gynai* "woman" implies both respect and endearment. In fact, the use of "woman" indicates more affection, than if Jesus had used the more formal word "mother." This may seem incredible to us, but we must never make the fatal mistake of judging other languages by our own.

Not only words and historical settings reveal hidden truths, but even grammatical forms may throw fresh light upon some otherwise unrecognized reality. For the ancient philosopher and priest of esoteric cults, steeped in the tradition of Classical Greek, the grammatical forms in the Lord's Prayer would seem almost rude. One does not find the optative forms of polite petition so characteristic of elaborate requests made to earthly and heavenly potentates. Rather than employing such august forms, the Christians made their requests to God in what seem to be blunt imperatives. This does not mean that Christians lacked respect for their heavenly Father, but it does mean that they were consistent with a new understanding of him. In the tens of thousands of papyri fragments which have been rescued from the rubbish heaps of the ancient Greek world, one finds the imperative forms used constantly between members of a family. When the Christians addressed God as "Father," it was perfectly natural therefore for them to talk to him as intimately as they would to their own father.

Unfortunately, the history of our own English language has almost reversed this process. Originally, men used "thou" and "thee" in prayer because it was the appropriate familiar form of address, but now these words have become relegated to prayer alone. However, to those who have not been raised in the atmosphere of the church and Sunday School such forms seem awkward and artificial. It is interesting to note how many people are beginning to pray to God with the pronoun "You." In doing this, they

are following the New Testament principle, which makes little or
no use of the high-flown artificial Asian style of Greek, but presents
its sublime message in the words of common men. Repeatedly
the church is called upon to cast aside the shackles of a tradition
abounding in words of empty meaning. Whenever it addresses itself
to living men in living words, faith is made alive by the Spirit
of God.

The Bible translator soon becomes profoundly aware of the
essential unity of his task. He may have begun by thinking of
the New and Old Testaments as separate compartments of revelation, but his judgment will soon be modified, for there are only
four short books of the New Testament (Philemon and 1-3 John)
in which one does not find quotations from the Old. In Revelation
there are more than 450 Old Testament quotations and allusions,
and the books of Matthew, Acts, Luke, and Hebrews each have
more than 100 quotations, often consisting of as much as several
verses. The books which are most often quoted in the New Testament are Psalms (186 times), Isaiah (177 times), Exodus (91 times),
Genesis (79 times), Ezekiel (63 times), and Jeremiah (55 times).
In fact there are only four books of the Old Testament which are
not quoted in the New: Ruth, Ezra, Ecclesiastes, and the Song
of Solomon.[1] The unity of Scripture does not stop with quotations,
for there are great themes which unite the sixty-six books of the
Bible into one revelation. Words such as "covenant," "grace,"
"sacrifice," "love," "mercy," "redemption," "joy," "peace," "salvation," "holy," and "judgment" bind the Scriptures together in one
indissoluble whole. A translator cannot correctly decide upon words
for the New Testament without bearing in mind what he must
use in the Old.

We must be careful not to think that translating is too easy
a task, nor must we be unduly frightened by the magnitude of
the many difficulties. Translating the Bible is not the work of a

[1] These figures are based upon the Appendix to the Nestle Greek New Testament, 20th
edition.

few weeks or months. It is the task of years, and often of a lifetime. However, two of the most difficult problems in translating usually remain quite unnoticed by the amateur or the untrained student. One of these perplexing difficulties is what to do with Paul's long sentences. They are not utterly impossible in English, for we can have long, involved sentences with many dependent clauses though that is not our usual manner of speaking. However, in languages which are utterly different from Indo-European ones, the translator finds that he must often completely revamp the involved sentence structures which are so familiar in the writings of Paul. One receives the impression that this great missionary pioneer, founder of churches, and apostle to the Gentiles, was at times so full of his subject that he simply could not find appropriate stopping places, and yet his sentences are not abnormally long in comparison with other Greek writers. Nevertheless, it is no easy task to take apart these linguistic monuments of clauses heaped one upon the other in intricately related positions and at the same time to preserve the meaningful relationships among these foundation truths of Christianity.

Another exasperating problem for the Bible translator and exegete is the Hebrew use of the tenses of the verb. Perhaps we should not even call the Hebrew forms different tenses, for they do not primarily signify different times of the action, but different kinds. Traditionally, the two principal sets of forms of the verb have been known as Imperfective and Perfective. And they correspond roughly to incomplete and complete action. Generally, the imperfective corresponds to our present and future tenses while the perfective is translated by our past, but there are many exceptions. Furthermore, when a perfective verb occurs in the first clause and the following clauses are joined by a Hebrew particle called *waw*, then the imperfective has the same value as the perfective in the first clause. Similarly, an initial perfective verb may be followed by imperfectives introduced by *waw*. Now, to make the situation even more complicated—when the prophet speaks of the future he always uses the perfective, that is to say, he speaks of the future as though it had already been accomplished. The biblical interpreter is often confused, for it is hard to know when the writer is prophesying and when he is recounting the history of a people. For the most part the context makes it clear as to the meaning of the passage, but in some instances we are left with legitimate doubts, for we are unable to reconstruct the historical background with sufficient assurance.

The average reader of the Bible is likely to be troubled by differences in the manuscripts, which result in quite different trans-lations of old familiar verses. When this happens our first reaction is generally a sense of loss. We have come to love the traditional rendering; and since it has been a part of our former religious experience, we assume that any change would only destroy the significance and spiritual content of the verse for us. When we read Romans 8:28 in the Revised Standard Version (1946), we find that "in everything God works for good with those who love him." We are told in a footnote that our older favorite rendering "all things work together for good" is a possible interpretation, but there is a sense in which we seem to prefer the older form, even as we feel more at home with old friends than with more recent ones. Jesus himself explained man's inevitable longing for tradition by the pointed parable about those who had drunk the old wine and did not appreciate the new wine, for they declared, "The old is better" (Luke 5:39).

But we should not pass by these better attested renderings without examining them. It is possible that we may have missed some spiritual truth. While holding to our former understanding of a matter we may rob ourselves of rich insight. It is not enough for us to argue that we must of course accept the "better rendering" because it is more "scholarly" or more "scientific." Religion is so largely a matter of the heart that we are unlikely to accept new interpretations unless we test them by their value in the light of Christian experience. We should look at these two renderings of

Romans 8:28 again. What is the basic difference? In the one, "All things work together for good," and in the other it is God who is working these things for our good. In the first there is a kind of blind fatalism which seems to imply an impersonal background to existence. In the second there is an emphatic declaration that a personal God is the basis of our Christian life and experience. The first interpretation sometimes leads to reckless exploits, the second provides the basis of quieting assurance.

In 1 John 5:18 we are accustomed to the translation, "We know that whosoever is born of God sinneth not; but he that is begotten of God keepeth himself, and that wicked one toucheth him not." It may be a surprise to find that in the Revised Standard Version this verse is translated, "We know that any one born of God does not sin, but He who was born of God keeps him, and the evil one does not touch him." The contrasts in meaning between these two translations are vast, but in Greek the only difference is the absence of a single small letter, making the difference between "himself" and "him." The older rendering states a truth which is manifestly contradicted by our experience and other Scripture. We as Christians are not able to keep ourselves. But we immediately recognize the truth of this newer rendering. We are not entrusted with the task of keeping ourselves, but "He who was born of God [that is, Jesus Christ] keeps us." This is the ministry of the resurrected Lord, who by his Spirit, sustains his redeemed. The grace of God does not stop with salvation, but becomes the basis of sanctification as well.

Some phrases in the King James Version are almost impossible to understand correctly since the Greek text which was available in the seventeenth century was so obviously faulty. In 1 Corinthians 8:7 we encounter the phrase "conscience of the idol." What can this mean? Does the Bible imply that an idol has a conscience? This would surely not be in keeping with the teachings of Scripture. It is similarly not "consciousness of the idol." In certain manuscripts two Greek words were confused; one meaning "conscience" and the other "experience." Once we understand this, the textual problem is settled; and we can fully appreciate the great improvement in the Revised Standard Version, "But some, through being hitherto accustomed to idols, eat food as really offered to an idol."

In some cases a difference of translation does not reflect a better manuscript evidence, that is to say, it does not mean that some earlier manuscript has been found which has a more correct wording, but we see more clearly now what is the meaning of the original. In Romans 1:17 we are accustomed to finding the words, "The just shall live by faith." This declaration has been a clarion call to faith and has been the text for many a sermon on the necessity of continued faith throughout life. It is true that this verse may have this meaning, but it is more probable that it means, "He who through faith is righteous shall live." This is in keeping with the whole emphasis of Paul throughout Romans, which has as its theme "justification by faith" (Rom. 5:1). Paul does not present two themes in Romans: the one "living by faith" and the other "justification by faith." His purpose was to emphasize one great primary truth of Christian doctrine: the righteousness which comes by faith in God. It is a kind of imputed righteousness, which has its origin in the grace of God and its response in the faith of man. Not only is this translation more in keeping with the Pauline context, but it is more faithful to the Hebrew of Habakkuk 2:4, of which it is a quotation.

For the average laymen and for some theological students, Greek is regarded as "quite impossible" and Hebrew is simply "for another world." For the Bible translator who wishes to do his work well, they become a daily necessity, which constantly enhance the value and effectiveness of the translation and reward the translator with some of his most priceless spiritual experiences.

3. Better Known English Translations

King James Version **1611**

The King James Version of the Bible is by far the most widely circulated translation in English. In fact, with all of the publicity given other translations in recent years, it likely still outnumbers all other English translations combined in total circulation. The stature or status of this translation in the English-speaking world can be seen, for example, in the fact that other translations justify their existence by explicit or implied criticism of it. It is the giant against which all others contend.

This well-loved translation was produced in England between 1604 and 1611 by a carefully selected group of Church of England scholars. Since it was sponsored by James I, King of England, it sometimes is referred to as the "Authorized Version," but this is not strictly accurate. No official or formal authorization appears to have been issued. The prestige of the king and the appeal of the translation itself are its sources of authority.

James I was a tyrant of less than heroic stature. It is ironic that this celebrated work stands as a memorial to a king who is remembered for little else. The value of the translation, of course, does not depend on the fact that the king sponsored it but on the careful work of the men who made it. The scholars who did the work made use of the best resources available at the time. They also

brought to their work a grandeur of literary style that has continued
to influence English usage ever since.

The King James text.—As summarized elsewhere in this book,
the nineteenth century produced pressure for new translations
because of the discovery of more reliable texts of the Greek New
Testament. This work was of tremendous interest to trained Bible
scholars, and its continued validity should not be overlooked.

The remarkable fact, however, is that study of the Greek text
in the main confirmed rather than discredited the King James
Version. Many little details in the King James stand to be corrected
by textual research, but no major teaching is altered.

The most striking changes proposed by nineteenth-century study
are the omission of a few passages, particularly the conclusion of
the Gospel of Mark and the story in the Gospel of John of the
woman taken in adultery.

The ending of Mark (16:9-20), as it appears in the King James
Version, seems to be a late addition supplied because the original
ending of the Gospel was somehow lost. One verse in this ending
(16:18) has been misinterpreted by the snake-handling cults of
the Southern mountains as the justification for their practices. Yet
this cannot fairly be blamed on the King James Version. Millions
of Christians have believed and studied it without reaching the
snake-handlers' conclusions.

The familiar story of the woman taken in adultery (John 7:53
to 8:11) almost surely does not belong in the Gospel of John. Yet
Bible scholars who agree on this also agree that it is a true incident
from the life of Jesus that belongs somewhere in the New Testament,
perhaps following Luke 21:38.

The King James text, then, is a legitimate problem but not one
that substantially discredits the version.

The King James language.—The language of the King James
Version is at once its glory and its stumbling block. Millions of
Christians have memorized long or short passages from this transla-
tion. Because the phrasing is so striking, it lends itself to memory

more readily than the more prosaic wording of other translations does. The majesty of the King James statement of familiar passages such as Genesis 1, Psalm 23, Matthew 5–7, and 1 Corinthians 13 cannot be matched elsewhere. How elevated—and elevating—for example, is Psalm 139:9-10: "If I take the wings of the morning, and dwell in the uttermost parts of the sea; even there shall thy hand lead me, and thy right hand shall hold me."

Given such beauty and such familiarity, it is not surprising that many of the pastors whose statements about Bible translations appear later in the book express a preference for the King James Version.

In the New Testament particularly, however, the grand style may obscure rather than clarify. The everyday Greek of the New Testament was a language designed to convey meaning, not merely mood. Grandeur of language has its place in human communication, but it is not always the best vehicle. The New Testament is concerned with message; it is written in a tone of urgency. Its purposes are not well served by the attitude of one Christian woman who said, "I like the King James Version because it sounds so mysterious."

What is meant, for example, by "another man's line of things made ready to our hand" (2 Cor. 10:16)? How many potential Christians have been baffled by such verb forms as "wist" and "wot"? Are we allowing the familiar and well-loved, which we have learned to understand, turn away from the Bible some to whom it is unfamiliar and confusing?

It is not the purpose of this book to convince anyone that the King James Version should be discarded. The version is a true treasure of English-speaking Christianity. The appeal here is that it be supplemented by other versions that are clearer and more contemporary in tone, even as the New Testament at the outset was clear and contemporary.

American Standard Version 1901

The American Standard Version was published in 1901. It was not a new translation but an American version of the English Revised Version published in 1885. Although the ERV New Testament received a great deal of attention and sold well when released in 1881, it was soon being criticized on both sides of the Atlantic. It was more accurate than the King James Version but did not read as well. The most famous preacher of the day, Charles Haddon Spurgeon, said the ERV was "strong in Greek, weak in English." The American Committee which had worked on this version decided that its translation preferences at various points should be included in the text of an American edition. Also, it wanted to eliminate antiquated words and replace purely British words with words more familiar to American readers. By previous agreement with the British university presses, the American version could not be published in less than fourteen years after the ERV was released. The American Standard Version had better acceptance in this country than the ERV had in England. It has been widely used for college and seminary study especially.

The New Testament in Modern Speech

The New Testament in Modern Speech by Richard F. Weymouth was published in England in 1903. As a teacher at Mill Hill School and Fellow of University College, London, Mr. Weymouth had studied both the Greek and English languages for more than sixty years. In his translation his first purpose was "to ascertain the exact meaning of every passage" using an up-to-date Greek text. His next step was "to consider how it could be most accurately and naturally exhibited in the English of the present day; in other words, how we can with some approach to probability suppose that the inspired writer himself would have expressed his thoughts, had he been writing in our age and country." Then he compared his work with other translations. In the Preface (from which these quotations have been borrowed) Mr. Weymouth made it very clear that his work was a translation from the Greek and not in any sense a revision of any other translation. On the other hand, he did not intend for his work to take the place of the popular and beloved versions. "His desire has rather been to furnish a succinct and compressed running commentary (not doctrinal) to be used side by side with its elder compeers."

Although the Weymouth translation was not widely popular, it went through numerous printings; the fifth edition with many improvements and added notes appeared in 1930. An American edition was published in 1943. Readers of Weymouth have appreciated his thorough scholarship as well as his skill with idiomatic modern English.

Centenary Translation of the New Testament

1924

Centenary Translation of the New Testament by Helen Barrett Montgomery was published in 1924 by the American Baptist Publication Society. The basic aim described in the Introduction by Mrs. Montgomery was: "To make a translation chiefly designed for the ordinary reader, intended to remove the veil that a literary or formal translation inevitably puts between the reader of only average education and the meaning of the text." To that end, the clear and accurate translation is aided by readable type, modern punctuation, and chapter titles and paragraph headings for quick recognition of contents. Mrs. Montgomery was an able and popular writer and speaker, especially on world missions. In 1921 she was president of the Northern Baptist Convention.

The Bible: A New Translation

The Bible: A New Translation by James Moffatt was published in 1926. The New Testament had appeared first in Edinburgh in 1913, and the Old Testament came out in 1924. A complete revised edition of the whole Bible was published in 1935, after Dr. Moffatt had evaluated many criticisms and suggestions. He wrote in the Introduction to the first edition: "The aim I have endeavoured to keep before my mind in making this translation has been to present the books of the Old and New Testament in effective, intelligible English. . . . The ideal of a translator is to let the readers enjoy part of that pleasure which the original once afforded to its audience in some far-off century, and I venture to hope that this translation may occasionally give such pleasure, in some degree, to those who cannot consult the Hebrew and Greek scriptures. To the best of my ability I have tried to be exact and idiomatic." Realizing that the writers of Bible books had used the ordinary language of the day to report the experiences of the people and God-given insights, Moffatt used the English of his time with remarkable skill to make the Word of God lively and vibrant. The translation was widely honored for Dr. Moffatt's scholarship as well as his contemporary English style.

The Bible, An American Translation

The Bible, An American Translation was published in 1931. It was a combination of two earlier works. *The New Testament, An American Translation* by Edgar J. Goodspeed had been released in 1923, and in 1927 had come *The Old Testament, An American Translation* by four translators under the editorship of J.M.P. Smith. Thus the combined volume has been known as the Smith-Goodspeed translation. In the Preface signed by both men they call attention to the rapid advance in learning that "has thrown new light upon every part of the Bible" and the changing English speech which is so different from "the sixteenth-century diction in which all our standard versions of it are clothed." Those facts were adequate reasons for a new translation "based upon the assured results of modern study, and put in the familiar language of today." The publisher aided their work considerably toward a "modern" impact by setting the material one column to the page, using modern punctuation, setting poetry as poetry, and moving chapter and verse numbers into the margin. The translation impressed readers with its vigor and boldness; it also had an American flavor that differentiated it from the Moffatt translation.

The New Testament in the Language of the People   1937

From some translations one gets the impression that the Bible was written in lofty Shakespearean English that might be appropriate if God spoke in an audible voice from a mountain top in a Cecil B. DeMille movie. Actually the New Testament was written in a simple, common language—Greek—which was clearly understandable to the people of the time. As Dr. Charles B. Williams stated in the introduction to this translation, only three of the New Testament books were written in what was considered literary Greek—Luke, Acts, and Hebrews. The rest were written in the simple Greek spoken by the everyday person of the time.

Because many translations were not written in the language of the people of the day, Dr. Williams, one of the original faculty members of Southwestern Baptist Seminary, felt the need to produce a translation which would be as understandable to modern English readers as the original Greek text was to the reader of the first century. In translating Luke, Acts, and Hebrews he used "good, smooth English." Elsewhere he translated the Greek into "simple everyday English which reproduces the everyday Greek which the writers used."

The result is a masterful translation that conveys simply and clearly to the modern reader the message of the New Testament as the first century reader understood it. Dr. Williams skillfully avoided the myopic vision that has plagued many individuals who have attempted to translate the New Testament. He considered carefully the viewpoints of others and came to well-thought-out decisions on difficult passages.

Obviously no translation can convey the complete meaning of any passage to every reader. It is important to compare various translations to gain a better understanding of any passage. Each translation has its own distinctive strong points that should be kept in mind. Since its appearance in 1937, Dr. Williams' *New Testament in the Language of the People* has been noted by laymen and scholars alike for its readability and accuracy. These distinctive strong points make it an invaluable aid in Bible study.

As Warren W. Wiersbe, pastor of Moody Memorial Church in Chicago, has said, "In a day when new translations keep appearing, few of them equal and none surpasses *The New Testament in the Language of the People.* The most experienced Bible student and the new Christian can use it with profit and delight. It is scholarly without being academic, and popular without being vulgar—a balance not found in many translations. For accuracy in the translation of the Greek verbs, it stands head and shoulders above the others. The more you use it, the more you appreciate it."

Dr. Williams' first aim was to make his translation clearly understandable. In the foreword to the first edition in 1937 he wrote: "Our aim is to make this greatest book in the world readable and understandable by the plain people. . . . In accord with this aim we have used practical everyday words to replace many technical religious and theological terms. In other words, we have tried to use the words and phrases that are understandable by the farmer and the fisherman, by the carpenter and the cowboy, by the cobbler and the cabdriver, by the merchant and the miner, by the milkmaid and the housemistress, by the woodcutter and the trucker. If these can understand it, it is certain that the scholar, the teacher, the minister, the lawyer, the doctor, and all others can."

The format has been designed in paragraph form so that the thought of the passages will not be lost in verse divisions and the reader can follow and understand easily. *The Presbyterian Journal* has said, "This volume is perfect for private and family devotions and for use in the pulpit. Dr. Williams has made God's Word extremely readable and hence meaningful in many places where one previously found it necessary to stop and ponder for a long time. The Williams translation should be used far more widely in evangelical circles."

But in producing this translation, Dr. Williams did not sacrifice scholarly research and accuracy to gain readability, as many modern translations and paraphrases have. He paid very careful attention to the actual Greek word meanings, word choice, and grammatical structure of the original Greek text. His careful attention to the Greek verb forms in particular has resulted in masterful translations of many difficult passages. An example of this is found in Matthew 16:19, where the translation reads, "Whatever you forbid on earth must be what is already forbidden in heaven, and whatever you permit on earth must be what is already permitted in heaven." This very accurately translates the Greek future perfect passive verbs in their grammatical context found in the Greek text.

As Philip C. Johnson, chairman of the department of biblical and theological studies at Gordon College, has said, "I know of no other English version that so consistently and clearly brings out the implications of the Greek tenses so important for a clear understanding of the Word."

Dr. Williams has also added numerous explanatory and scholarly footnotes to aid the reader in understanding the text. Brief introductions are also given at the beginning of each book, giving the author, occasion, theme, and audience of the writing.

The combination of readability with scholarly accuracy that Dr. Williams has achieved is evident in his translation of 1 Corinthians 13. Since the Greek text indicates that this passage was written in a Greek poetic form. Dr. Williams has translated it into a similar English form—blank verse, for instance:

> If I could speak the languages of men, of angels too,
> And have no love,
> I am only a rattling pan or a clashing cymbal.
> If I should have the gift of prophecy,
> And know all secret truths, and knowledge in its every form,
> And have such perfect faith that I could move mountains,
> But have no love, I am nothing.
> If I should dole out everything I have for charity,

And give my body up to torture in mere boasting pride,
But have no love, I get from it no good at all.
Love is so patient and so kind;
Love never boils with jealousy;
It never boasts, it is never puffed with pride;
It does not act with rudeness, or insist upon its rights;
It never gets provoked, it never harbors evil thoughts;
Is never glad when wrong is done,
But always glad when truth prevails;
It bears up under anything,
It exercises faith in everything,
It keeps up hope in everything,
It gives us power to endure in anything.

Not only is this passage very readable, it is also a precise and accurate translation of the Greek text. For example, the Greek word translated in the phrase, "they will *be set aside*" occurs several times in the passage and is given the same translation, as in the phrase, "I *laid aside.*" The word translated in the phrase "they *will cease,*" however, is an entirely different Greek word and is thus given a different translation, since its meaning is slightly different. This careful attention to the author's intent in word choice is an indication of the scholarly and detailed work that went into the preparation of this translation.

The best witness to the usefulness of this masterful translation has been its ability over the years to fulfill the original purpose Dr. Williams expressed for it in the foreword to the first edition, "May the face of Christ, who is the Theme of this book and the Light of the world, shine into the heart and upon the life of everyone who reads it."

Ken Mitchell
Moody Press

Revised Standard Version 1952

Something of the distinctive nature of the Revised Standard Version[1] is revealed in its origins. It was initiated and first authorized by the International Council of Religious Education on behalf of the forty evangelical denominations of the United States and Canada associated with the Council through their boards of education. All these denominations were represented in an Advisory Board of some fifty members charged with special responsibility for matters of general policy, finance, and public relations, who were consulted with respect to principles underlying the revision, and who reviewed drafts of the translation in process. The Standard Bible Committee which had first been appointed in 1929 was authorized to proceed with the work in 1937. It has the sole responsibility for the wording of the translation. The members of the Standard Bible Committee by 1952 had come from more than twenty theological seminaries and universities. It was, from the first, under the chairmanship of Dean Luther A. Weigle of Yale Divinity School, who continued to administer the office of the RSV Bible Committee until the autumn of 1970.

The publication of the Revised Standard Version was authorized in 1951 by the National Council of the Churches of Christ of the U.S.A., and the wide representation and participation in the project continued, inasmuch as educational boards of denominations not in the National Council remained in the Division of Christian Education, and the ecumenical character of the National Council was enlarged.

[1] See the Preface to the RSV (containing the Second Edition of the New Testament) 1971, and the Preface to the *RSV Common Bible*, 1973. See also Millar Burrows, "The RSV of the Old Testament," *VT* Suppl. VII 1960, pp. 206-221; H. G. May, "The RSV Bible," *VT* XXIV 1974, pp. 238-240; Editor Luther A. Weigle, *Introduction to the RSV of the New Testament*, by the members of the revision committee, Nelson's 1956, *Introduction to the RSV of the Old Testament* by the members of the revision committee, Nelson's 1952; Millar Burrows, *Diligently Compared: The RSV and KJV Old Testament*, Nelson's 1964; R. Bridges and L. A. Weigle, *The Bible Word Book*, Nelson's 1960; H. G. May, "The RSV After 20 Years," *McCormick Quarterly* 1966, pp. 301-308.

The New Testament was published in 1946. On St. Jerome's Day, September 30, 1952, the appearance of the complete RSV Bible was celebrated by two million Protestants participating in 3,200 interdenominational worship services at which outstanding church leaders spoke. The first copy off the press was presented by Dean Weigle to President Truman, and the celebration began with a national observance at Washington in the National Guard Armory, which some 8,000 attended.

The RSV Bible, in contrast with most of the other recent translations, is not a new Bible. It is an authorized revision of the American Standard Version published in 1901, which was a revision of the English Revised Version of 1881-1885, which was a revision of the King James Version. It is described in the Preface as a translation which "seeks to preserve all that is best in the English Bible as it has been known and used through the years, designed for use in public and private worship, and preserving those qualities which have given to the KJV a supreme place in English literature." A common slogan associated with the first publicity was, "The Word of Life in Living Language."

The Translation Committee in charge of the RSV text has recommended revisions and other projects in the translation of the Bible or related books. In spite of certain restraints laid upon the translators, the RSV came closer to being a new translation than might have been expected, being a much more thorough revision than either the ERV or the ASV, for the language was generally adjusted to modern usage (see Burrows, pp. 209ff). Idiomatic English expressions replaced obsolete and archaic words and phrases to make a more readable translation, for example, KJV "let" used in the sense of "hinder" or "prevent"; "prevent" used in the sense of "come before"; "allow" meaning "approve"; "conversation" meaning "well-being"; etc. See Bridges and Weigle, *The Bible Word Book,* for articles on 827 obsolete and archaic phrases corrected in the RSV Bible.

The RSV is more literal and less paraphrastic than many of

the modern translations, attempting to indicate at the same time what the Hebrew and Greek texts say, and what they mean.[2]

The RSV as an authorized version is to be credited with breaking the ground for the later translations. It took the brunt of the attack from circles which now *welcome* "New Bibles." There were even some Bible burnings and predictions of an early demise of the RSV translation. Nevertheless, it found a welcome in the hearts of both conservative and liberal Christians.

Many of the denominational publishing houses as a matter of course use the RSV as their major text, relying on it for church school and general publications. It has been estimated that some 30 million copies have been sold. It inspired numerous publication projects, including commentaries, dictionaries, study Bibles, parallel Bibles, Synoptic parallels, interlinear Greek-English New Testaments, devotional manuals, concordances, maps, etc.

The consonantal Hebrew and Aramaic text revised in the 6th to the 9th centuries by the Masoretes was the basic text for the RSV Old Testament, and most of the corrections adopted were based on the ancient versions (Greek, Aramaic, Syriac, and Latin) or more recently discovered Hebrew texts. In each instance where such corrections were made, in contrast with most other modern translations, notes were added to every edition of the RSV indicating the source of the correction. In the case of the *New English Bible,* there is a Library Edition for students and scholars and L. H. Brockington's 269-page volume, *The Hebrew Text of the Old Testament, The Readings Adopted by the Translators of the New English Bible,* 1973, both of which indicate the changes from the Masoretic Text. See also the Textual Notes accompanying some editions of the *New American Bible.* The RSV was relatively conservative in its use of the versions.

The readings of the Old and New Testament sections of the

[2] See Amos 1:3 in RSV and NAB; contrast NEB, TEV. See Psalm 19:1 in NAB and RSV; contrast TEV. Contrast Psalm 23:3 in RSV and TEV. Contrast Matthew 5:3 in RSV and NAB with NEB, etc. Contrast Hebrews 11:1 in RSV (15 words) and The Living Bible (38 words).

Translation Committee were approved by formal vote after scholarly discussion and debate. During the last two and one-half years
of the work on the Old Testament before its publication in 1952,
the Old Testament section met for a total of 140 long days.

The RSV differs from its previous authorized versions by the
fact that it has a continuing committee, which is still active. At
the request of the General Convention of the Protestant Episcopal
Church, in 1957 there appeared the Old Testament Apocrypha.
In 1959, in response to criticisms and suggestions from various
readers, a few changes were authorized for subsequent editions,
most of them corrections in punctuation, capitalization, or footnotes,
while others were changes in words or phrases made in the interest
of clarity or accuracy of translation.

In 1965-66 the RSV Catholic Edition was prepared by the Catholic Biblical Association of Great Britain, and edited by two of its
members, Dom Bernard Orchard and the Rev. Reginald C. Fuller,
who were later to become members of the RSV Bible Committee.
There were no changes in the Old Testament text, but a number
of changes, believed to be necessary for theological or liturgical
reasons, were made in the New Testament text and were carefully
noted in an appendix. The Old Testament Deuterocanonical Books
were placed among the Old Testament Books, in accord with
Catholic usage. The foreword for the American edition was prepared by His Eminence, Richard Cardinal Cushing of Boston.

In 1965 Richard Cardinal Cushing granted an *imprimatur* to a
popular annotated study edition of the RSV Bible with the Apocrypha, published by the Oxford University Press, and of which a
new edition has just appeared. It was the first translation of the
English Bible to have both Catholic and Protestant approval. In
matters of translation there need be no differences along confes-
sional lines.

In 1971 there was published the second edition of the New
Testament, which is found in the more recent printings of the RSV
Bible, including among others the *Concordia Bible with Notes—New*

Testament RSV, by Martin H. Franzmann, the *New Oxford Annotated Bible, Harper's Study Bible,* the *RSV Common Bible,* and
Zondervan's *The Layman's Parallel Bible.* The second edition profits
from textual and linguistic studies since the RSV New Testament
was first issued in 1946. Many proposals for modification were
submitted to the Committee by individuals and by two evangelical
denominational committees, namely the Advisory Board on English
Versions of the Lutheran Church (Missouri Synod), and the RSV
Study Committee of the Christian Reformed Church. In the second
edition the longer ending of Mark (16:9-20) and the pericope of
the adulterous woman are restored to the text, accompanied by
informative footnotes. With the support of the Bodmer Papyrus
XIV in Luke 24:51*a* the words "and carried up into heaven" are
restored to the text. Likewise Luke 22:19*b*-20 in the Lucan account
of the Last Supper is restored to the text for reasons given in Bruce
Metzger, *A Textual Commentary on the Greek New Testament, A
Companion Volume to the UBS's Greek New Testament* (third edition) 1971, pp. 173-177. Two of the five editors of the forthcoming
third edition of the UBS's *Greek New Testament* are on the RSV
Committee.

The *RSV Common Bible* appeared in 1973 with a special arrangement of the Old Testament Apocrypha books which recognizes
the differences in the respective canons of Roman Catholics, Orthodox, and Protestants. Arranged in the order more familiar to Roman
Catholics, but placed between the Testaments, the Old Testament
Apocrypha books (Tobit, Judith, the Additions to the Book of
Esther, Wisdom of Solomon, Sirach or Ecclesiasticus, Baruch, Letter
of Jeremiah [Baruch chapter 6], the Additions to the Book of Daniel,
1 Maccabees, 2 Maccabees) are separated from the remaining books
of the Apocrypha (1 and 2 Esdras and the Prayer of Manasseh)
by a blank page and a notation that 1 Esdras and the Prayer of
Manasseh are included in the Greek canon. The longer Greek canon
is explained in the Preface, and a subcommittee of the RSV Bible
Committee under the chairmanship of Professor Bruce M. Metzger

is engaged in translating 3 and 4 Maccabees and Psalm 151 so that the complete Greek canon may be represented in the *RSV Common Bible*, a project suggested by Archbishop Athenagoras II and approved by Archbishop Iakovos.

As the Preface states, the *RSV Common* (Ecumenical) *Bible* was approved by the Division of Christian Education of the National Council of the Churches of Christ with its special arrangement of the Apocrypha-Deuterocanonical Books, not to preempt the title, but in recognition of our common biblical heritage. It is hoped that the arrangement may serve as a precedent for other ecumenical editions.

The RSV Bible Committee continues its work as an increasingly ecumenical and international committee with membership drawn from the U.S., Canada, and England, and currently with Roman Catholic, Protestant, Jewish, and Greek Orthodox representation. Besides the new Apocrypha project just mentioned, it is working towards the second edition of the RSV Old Testament and is at the same time engaged in a thorough, overall survey of the RSV Bible, in part to take advantage of the recent advances made in studies in Hebrew grammar and lexicography,[3] Septuagint studies and the transmission of the Hebrew text, Ugarit,[4] and Qumran.[5]

> Herbert G. May, chairman
> Revised Standard Version Bible Committee
> National Council of Churches of Christ

---

[3] See W. L. Moran. "The Hebrew Language in Its Northwest Semitic Background." *BANE*, 54ff.

[4] See W. L. Moran, M. Dahood, M. H. Pope, *et al.*

[5] See P. W. Skehan, *BA*, XXVIII, 87ff.; F. M. Cross. "Ancient Library of Qumran." *HTR*, LVII, 281ff.; J. G. Janzen, *HSM*, #6; P. W. Skehan and H. M. Orlinsky. articles in *JBL*, LXXVIII, 21ff.

The New Testament in Modern English

TRANSLATOR'S FOREWORD*

There seem to be three necessary tests which any work of transference from one language to another must pass before it can be classed as good translation. The first is simply that it must not sound like a translation at all. If it is skillfully done, and we are not previously informed, we should be quite unaware that it *is* a translation, even though the work we are reading is far distant from us in both time and place. That is a first, and indeed fundamental test, but it is not by itself sufficient. For the translator himself may be a skillful writer, and although he may have conveyed the essential meaning, characterization and plot of the original author, he may have so strong a style of his own that he completely changes that of the original author. I would therefore make this the second test: that a translator does his work with the least possible obtrusion of his own personality. The third and final test which a good translator should be able to pass is that of being able to produce in the hearts and minds of his readers an effect equivalent to that produced by the author upon his original readers. Of course no translator living would claim that his work successfully achieved these three ideals. But he must bear them in mind constantly as principles for his guidance.

As I have frequently said, a translator is not a commentator. He is usually well aware of the different connotations which a certain passage may bear, but unless his work is to be cluttered with footnotes he is bound, after careful consideration, to set down what is the most likely meaning. Occasionally one is driven into

*This material is from *The New Testament in Modern English* (Revised Edition) by J. B. Phillips (copyright by J. B. Phillips 1958, 1960, 1972) and is being used by permission of Macmillan Publishing Co.

what appears to be a paraphrase, simply because a literal translation of the original Greek would prove unintelligible. But where this has proved necessary I have always been careful to avoid giving any slant or flavor which is purely of my own making. That is why I have been rather reluctant to accept the suggestion that my translation is "interpretation"! If the word interpretation is used in a bad sense, that is, if it is meant that a work is tendentious, or that there has been a manipulation of the words of New Testament Scripture to fit some private point of view, then I would still strongly repudiate the charge! But "interpretation" can also mean transmitting meaning from one language to another, and skilled interpreters in world affairs do not intentionally inject any meaning of their own. In this sense I gladly accept the word interpretation to describe my work. For, as I see it, the translator's function is to understand as fully and deeply as possible what the New Testament writers had to say and then, after a process of what might be called reflective digestion, to write it down in the language of the people today. . . .

After reading a large number of commentaries I have a feeling that some scholars, at least, have lived so close to the Greek Text that they have forgotten their sense of proportion. I doubt very much whether the New Testament writers were as subtle or as self-conscious as some commentators would make them appear. For the most part I am convinced that they had no idea that they were writing Holy Scripture. They would be, or indeed perhaps are, amazed to learn what meanings are sometimes read back into their simple utterances! Paul, for instance, writing in haste and urgency to some of his wayward and difficult Christians, was not tremendously concerned about dotting the i's and crossing the t's of his message. I doubt very much whether he was even concerned about being completely consistent with what he had already written. Consequently, it seems to me quite beside the point to study his writings microscopically, as it were, and deduce hidden meanings of which almost certainly he was unaware. His letters are alive,

and they are moving—in both senses of that word—and their meaning can no more be appreciated by cold minute examination than
can the beauty of a bird's flight be appreciated by dissection after
its death. We have to take these living New Testament documents
in their context, a context of supreme urgency and often of acute
danger. But a word is modified very considerably by the context
in which it appears, and where a translator fails to realize this,
we are not far away from the result of an electronic word trans-
muter! . . .

I feel strongly that a translator, although he must make himself
as familiar as possible with New Testament Greek usage, must
steadfastly refuse to be driven by the bogey of consistency. He
must be guided both by the context in which a word appears,
and by the sensibilities of modern English readers. In the story
of the raising of Lazarus, for example, Martha's objection to opening the grave would be natural enough to an Eastern mind. But
to put into her lips the words, "by this time he's stinking," would
sound to Western ears unpleasantly out of key with the rest of
that moving story. . . .

Perhaps a few words about the kind of technique which I have
adopted may be introduced here. I have found imaginative sympa-
thy, not so much with words as with people, to be essential. If
it is not presumptuous to say so, I attempted, as far as I could,
to think myself into the heart and mind of Paul, for example,
or of Mark or of John the Divine. Then I tried further to imagine
myself as each of the New Testament authors writing his particular
message for the people of today. No one could succeed in doing
this superlatively well, if only because of the scantiness of our
knowledge of the first century A.D. But this has been my ideal,
and that is why consistency and meticulous accuracy have sometimes both been sacrificed in the attempt to transmit freshness and
life across the centuries. The cross-headings which appear throughout the book are meant to make it both more readable and more
intelligible; at the same time they are intended to be quite unob-

trusive and can easily be ignored. But, by the use of these headings, solid and rather forbidding slabs of continuous writing (such as appear in the Greek Text) are made more assimilable to the modern reader, whose reading habits have already been "conditioned" by the comparatively recent usage of clear punctuation, intelligent paragraphing and good printer's type.

Although I have worked directly in this translation from the best available Greek Text, it would be ungracious to forget the very many people who have made the work possible. I think first of the textual critics, whose patient work gives us a text to work from which is as near as possible to that of the original writers. I am most grateful to them, as all translators must be, and I should also like to express my thanks to the numerous commentators whose works I have consulted again and again. . . . Although it would be impossible to supply a full list, I am extremely grateful to the many people—including first-rate scholars, hard-working parish priests, busy ministers, doctors, scientists, missionaries, education-ists, elderly saints and lively young people—who have, over the years, written me hundreds of letters, the great majority of which were constructive and useful. Their help has been invaluable.

It has been my practice not to consult other modern translations until my own version has been finished. I do not therefore owe anything directly to any contemporary translator, much as I admire the work of Dr. J. W. C. Wand and Dr. E. V. Rieu of this country, and Dr. Edgar J. Goodspeed of the United States of America. But none of us who translates today can be unaware of the trail that was blazed for us near the beginning of this century by such pioneers as Dr. R. F. Weymouth and Dr. James Moffatt. We cannot but admit that we are in a much more favorable position because such men had the courage to break a centuries-old tradition, and translate into contemporary English. . . .

The Holy Bible: The Berkeley Version in Modern English 1959

The Holy Bible: The Berkeley Version in Modern English was published in 1959. Gerrit Verkuyl was editor-in-chief and translator of the New Testament. A staff of twenty translators worked on the Old Testament; they represented a variety of denominations, colleges, and seminaries. Not only is this a completely new translation from the original languages, but Dr. Verkuyl in the Preface asserts it is not a paraphrase, "for that leads so readily to the infusion of human thought with divine revelation, to the confusion of the reader. Instead of paraphrasing, we offer brief notes, related to, but apart from, the inspired writings, to clarify and to give a sharper view of the message." Besides its English of current usage, the translation also attempts to aid the reader with the liberal use of Arabic numerals, modern terminology for weights and measures, and frequent notations of dating.

The Amplified Bible

The Amplified Bible is the product of years of extensive research by biblical scholars whose primary aim was to faithfully present the full meaning of the key words in the original texts. This amplification of key words assists the English reader in understanding what is readily understood by the Hebrew, Aramaic, and Greek reader. A word-for-word translation is recognized to be inadequate at times, losing the shades of meaning intended in the original language. By amplifying these areas to clarify the meaning, English readers may more readily grasp the full intent of the writers. The contribution of Frances E. Siewert, B. Lit., B.D., M.A., D. Lit., as Research Secretary is especially outstanding.

The Amplified Gospel of John was introduced in 1954, followed by the complete New Testament, published by the Lockman Foundation and Zondervan Publishing House in 1958. The Amplified Old Testament was brought out in two parts: Part Two (Job-Malachi) in 1962, and Part One (Genesis-Esther) in 1964. The entire *Amplified Bible,* combining all these parts into one volume, was published by Zondervan in 1965.

The format of the *Amplified Bible* is a standard two-column page, and each verse is indented as a paragraph. Cross references are found in brackets after the text. Notes and explanatory comments are placed at the bottom of the page, and most of the notes, especially in the New Testament, provide the source for the translation or amplification. Sources most frequently referred to are Vincent, Thayer, and Cremer.

Throughout the *Amplified Bible* arbitrary punctuation is used to identify various forms of textual expansion. The explanation is found in the front of the book, and there are four basic types:
1. Parentheses ( ) and Dashes — : signify additional phases of meaning included in the original word, phrase, or clause of the original language.

2. Titles of Deity: are set off only with commas.
3. Brackets [ ]: contain justified clarifying words or comments not actually expressed in the immediate original text.
4. Italics: point out certain familiar passages now recognized as not adequately supported by the original manuscripts. Also "and," "or" and other connectives in italics indicate that the word itself is not in the original text, but it is used to connect additional English words indicated in the same original word.

A familiar sample passage will illustrate the translation's format and reading style. The following passage is John 3:1-6, 12-16.

NOW there was a certain man among the Pharisees named Nicodemus, a ruler—a leader, an authority—among the Jews;

2 Who came to Jesus at night and said to Him, Rabbi, we know *and* are certain that You are come from God [as] a Teacher; for no one can do these signs—these wonderworks, these miracles, and produce the proofs—that You do, unless God is with him.

3 Jesus answered him, I assure you, most solemnly I tell you, that unless a person is born again (anew, from above), he cannot ever see—know, be acquainted with [and experience]—the kingdom of God.

4 Nicodemus said to Him, How can a man be born when he is old? Can he enter his mother's womb again, and be born?

5 Jesus answered, I assure you, most solemnly I tell you, except a man be born of water and (ᵐeven) the Spirit, he cannot [ever] enter the kingdom of God. [Ezek. 36:25-27.]

6 What is born of [from] the flesh is flesh—of the physical is physical; and what is born of the Spirit is spirit.

12 If I have told you of things that happen right here on the earth, and yet none of you believes Me, how can you believe—trust Me, adhere to Me, rely on Me—if I tell you of heavenly things?

13 And yet no one has ever gone up to heaven; but there is One Who has come down from heaven, the Son of man [Himself], *Who is—dwells, Whose home is—in heaven.*

14 And just as Moses lifted up the serpent in the desert [on a pole], so must—so it is necessary that—the Son of man be lifted up [on the cross]; Num. 21:9.

15 In order that every one who believes in Him—who cleaves to Him, trusts Him and relies on Him—may *not perish, but* have

eternal life *and* [actually] live forever!

16 For God so greatly loved *and* dearly prized the world that He [even] gave up His only-begotten ([n]unique) Son, so that whoever believes in (trusts, clings to, relies on) Him shall not perish—come to destruction, be lost—but have eternal (everlasting) life.

m) "Kai" may be rendered "even."
n) Moulton and Milligan.

The fourfold aim of the *Amplified Bible,* expressed in the Preface, is:

1. It should be true to the original languages.
2. It should be grammatically correct.
3. It should be understandable to the masses.
4. It should give the Lord Jesus Christ his proper place which the Word gives him. No word will be personalized.

On the basis of these aims, the *Amplified Bible* has attempted to progress beyond the point of a word-for-word translation and to offer to the reader the full meaning revealed in the original tongues.

Dr. W. A. Criswell, pastor of the First Baptist Church, Dallas, Texas, has said: "With increasing frequency, I hear our people use and teach from the *Amplified Bible.* . . . They find in its pages the true meaning of the Scriptures, in a way they could discover in no other place. The *Amplified Bible* makes the Word of God live for the people."

Ronald W. Haynes
Zondervan Publishing Co.

The Jerusalem Bible

The Jerusalem Bible climaxes many decades of devoted scholarship, beginning at the turn of the century when Father Marie-Joseph Lagrange, a French Dominican scholar, established L'Ecole Biblique, a small school for biblical studies in the city of Jerusalem. Over the years this institute developed into one of the leading centers of Bible study and research in the world.

As they studied the Scriptures, the men at L'Ecole Biblique felt that the crowning pinnacle of their efforts would be to produce a thoroughly modern version of the Bible, based on original sources, but making full use of all the latest developments of biblical scholarship and of the many revealing archaeological discoveries of recent times.

The culmination of these activities was a French translation of the Old and New Testaments published in 43 fascicles (separately bound sections) between 1948 and 1955. The *Bible de Jerusalem* is not only a superb translation; hand in hand with the text there is a running commentary in the form of explanatory notes, introductions to the various books of the Bible, and a system of cross references, all of which render the meaning of the Bible text more comprehensible to both the scholar and the general reader.

In 1956, the 43 fascicles were combined into the one-volume *Bible de Jerusalem* which, within a short time, became the most widely used Bible in the French-speaking world.

As soon as it was apparent that this was one of the great Bibles of all times, plans were set in motion to provide an equivalent English version. Invited to head this project was Father Alexander Jones, one of the world's leading biblical scholars. Father Jones enlisted the collaboration of a group of distinguished biblical and literary experts, and the project was under way. Work began in 1957.

Although based on the French *Bible de Jerusalem*, the English version is *not* simply a translation from the French. It is rather a direct translation from the ancient texts which accepts the interpretations adopted in the French version. In all cases, the original texts—the Hebrew Masoretic, the Greek Septuagint, and the Dead Sea Scrolls for the Old Testament, and the accepted Greek and Aramaic texts for the New Testament—were the ultimate source for the translation.

In the translation of *The Jerusalem Bible,* every precaution has been taken to assure the absolute accuracy of the text in the light of the most up-to-date biblical knowledge. At the same time, the English employed throughout is modern, fresh, vigorous, and meaningful to the modern reader.

All archaic expressions have been eliminated. Words whose meanings have changed with the passage of time—expressions found frequently in the Douay version and the King James Version, but no longer having relevance today—have been eliminated and more communicative modern phraseology used. *Thee, thou, art, mayest,* and such terms have been completely replaced by their modern equivalents.

Since English-speaking peoples have traditionally used the King James Version spelling of proper names in their literature and everyday language, it was decided after careful consideration that the KJV spelling of proper names would be adopted (Noah for *Noe,* Joshua for *Josue,* Jonah for *Jonas,* Messiah for *Messias,* etc.)— except in cases where modern linguistic research has resulted in more accurately spelled transliterations of the Hebrew or Greek.

Colloquialisms are strictly confined to their appropriate place, and contemporary slangy expressions are *avoided altogether;* so that we have not only a modern, fresh, vivid Bible, but one which also conveys the beauty and majesty of the original writings.

The value of the introductory essays and the running notes in *The Jerusalem Bible* cannot be overemphasized. Through this continuous commentary the reader learns the background against which biblical events took place. The people of Israel did not live in a vacuum, nor did the early Christians. Many incidents and customs mentioned in the Bible, many actions of Bible personalities are quite incomprehensible unless they can be related to the ancient civilizations and cultures surrounding the Palestine of those times. This is accomplished by the introductions.

The Dominican scholars who prepared these notes and introductions were fully aware of, and used in their own research, all the considerable advances that had been made in sciences which help to explain the Bible—the most recent archaeological findings, the application of the carbon method of dating, the unearthing of the Dead Sea Scrolls, and so on. Every conceivable new tool provided by modern research has been utilized to aid the reader's understanding of the Bible text. Thus the reader has a completely modern Bible translation and an excellent, up-to-the-minute commentary *combined in one convenient volume.*

It is the conviction of the publishers that *The Jerusalem Bible* is a truly ecumenical version of the Bible since its approach is objective, and it is free from any form of secular interpretation or doctrinal emphasis. That this conviction is more than a mere hope may be seen from the following remarks by prominent biblical scholars.

> Well known to scholars as an important contribution to biblical studies, *The Jerusalem Bible* now appears in an English translation. . . . It is an admirable demonstration of the informed and intelligent conservatism characteristic of Roman Catholic biblical scholarship, showing how closely Catholic, Protestant, and Jewish scholars agree in matters of textual, literary, and historical criticism, and thus affording an excellent instrument for the "ecumenical dialogue" now being undertaken. . . . The introductions and notes are not inspirational but informative; they are not, however, merely historical and literary but put foremost the religious purpose and significance of the text. They are definitely Christian without being at all sectarian.

> Dr. Millar Burrows
> *Professor Emeritus of Biblical Theology*
> *Divinity School, Yale University*

Although this translation from original sources has been made with scrupulous accuracy, the editors have contrived to find a language which sounds as fresh to modern ears as the Bible was to the first Christians. We have, in other words, a genuinely contemporary version of Holy Scripture.

John Cardinal Heenan
Archbishop of Westminster

The Jerusalem Bible provides a clear and dignified English translation along with scholarly introductions and helpful footnotes. Striking a balance between the literary and archaeological approaches, it is a good introduction for the general reader into biblical scholarship.

Dr. Cyrus H. Gordon
Professor of Near Eastern Studies
Brandeis University

John J. Delaney, Editor
Doubleday and Company

Today's English Version

The New Testament in Today's English Version was published by the American Bible Society in September, 1966; the complete Bible is scheduled for publication in early 1976. This translation, the first one to be prepared under the auspices of the American Bible Society, came in response to repeated proposals that a translation be made that would be understood by anyone who reads English, either as a native speaker of the language or as a foreigner. It was also felt that such a translation could meet the needs of non-Christian readers, and of readers with a limited level of formal education for whom the standard translations might be difficult to understand.

Dr. Robert G. Bratcher, a member of the Translations Department staff, was commissioned to prepare such a translation of the New Testament; he was assisted by other members of the staff, and by a Consultative Committee which was eventually appointed by the American Bible Society.

The TEV is a "common-language" translation, that is, it uses that part of the English language that is common to all who read and write it, irrespective of national origin or of level of formal education. The language is written, not spoken, and so conforms to the written style of English. Slang, regionalisms, and provincialisms are excluded, since the translation is intended for people everywhere. Technical terms and difficult polysyllabic words are avoided. The vocabulary is limited, but it is not artificially restricted, and account is taken of the difference in range between the vocabulary that a reader can produce and one that he can consume. People can understand more words than they themselves ordinarily use, that is, their consumer vocabulary is larger than their producer vocabulary. Where rarely used words or expressions must be used, what is called "redundant information" may be included in order to help the reader understand the word or expression in question.

For example, "myrrh" might not be a widely-known word; so "a drug called myrrh" (Mark 15:23) enables the reader to know what the word means. Careful attention is paid to the needs of the hearer, as distinct from those of the reader. This shows up especially in two aspects of the translation: homonyms and punctuation. In the former case, the lack of difference in sound between "hear" and "here," for example, requires that the context be such that the listener will know which word is being spoken; he cannot go back and look at the word, and so he must understand it clearly and unmistakably as soon as he hears it. The relation between phrases and clauses within the sentence must be immediately apparent, and the punctuation should be such as to avoid as much ambiguity as possible. Quite often this involves the rearrangement of information in a sentence, in order to achieve a chronological or logical progression of events or arguments, for greater ease of understanding.

The needs of readers who read and write English as a foreign language make it impossible to use idiomatic expressions very widely. Idioms are vivid and meaningful for native speakers of the language, but may be misleading or unintelligible for those who know it as a foreign tongue.

The TEV is also a "dynamic equivalence" translation, as contrasted with a "formal equivalence" translation, traditionally associated with standard versions of the Bible. Dr. Eugene A. Nida, the Executive Secretary of the Translations Department of the American Bible Society, has succinctly defined the principle of dynamic equivalence as follows: "To translate is to try to stimulate in the new readers in the new language the same reaction to the text as the one the original author wished to stimulate in his first and immediate readers." This means that no attempt is made always to translate a given Hebrew or Greek word by the same word in English; rather the TEV uses the English word or expression that most faithfully and naturally represents the meaning of the original word in the context in which it is used. Nor does the translation attempt to follow the word order or match the word classes of the original languages, but it seeks to express the meaning of the original as naturally as possible in English. As Ronald Knox, the brilliant British translator of the Bible from the Vulgate, has said: "A translation is good in proportion as you can forget, while reading it, that it is a translation at all."

One immediate consequence of the application of this principle is to divide the sometimes inordinately long and complicated sentences in Greek—which is very good Greek style—into shorter sentences in English. The eloquent opening of the book of Hebrews, for example, begins with a long and beautifully constructed sentence that is four verses long; the TEV divides this into four separate sentences. The intricate sentence in the Greek text of 1 Peter 1:3-5 is broken up into four complete sentences in English, and the extremely long sentence in Ephesians 1:3-14 becomes fourteen sentences in English. Rhetorical questions are an effective device, but they may be misunderstood in English as genuine questions. "What can a man give in return for his life?" (Mark 8:37) is not a request for information; it is a rhetorical way of saying, "There is nothing a man can give to regain his life." Similarly, for rhetorical effect, a statement of fact may be phrased in Greek as a condition, where no real condition is intended. For example, in Luke 11:20 we read: "If it is by the finger of God that I cast our demons, then the kingdom of God has come upon you." To avoid any ambiguity, this is translated, "It is rather by means of God's power that I drive out demons, which proves that the Kingdom of God has already come to you."

The translator's ideal is that the readers of his translation will understand the text as well as did the original readers of the original text. This ideal obviously cannot be reached completely because modern readers are separated from the original author and readers by a wide gap of time and difference in cultures. The Bible was not written by Americans in the twentieth century, and the gap between the two cultures cannot be bridged completely in the translation, since a faithful translation, as opposed to a loose para-phrase, accurately preserves the historical and cultural setting of the original text. Only a detailed commentary can supply all the information needed for a full understanding of the setting and meaning of the original text.

A dynamic equivalence translation takes into account another factor, which is sometimes misunderstood. The original writer and his readers shared a lot of information which underlies the written document, and which the writer did not have to elaborate or make explicit. He could take it for granted that his readers knew what he was talking about; thus, he did not have to explain in detail everything he said. But much, if sometimes not all, of this information is missing to the modern reader, and he is not sure of the exact meaning of the text. In 1 Corinthians 7:36-38, for example, our lack of specific information about the situation in Corinth makes it impossible to know what is the precise relationship between the man and the "virgin" referred to. William Barclay gives three different possible renderings of this passage. And in 1 Corinthians 11:10 the modern interpreter, unlike the original readers, does not understand precisely what Paul meant when he qualified his advice about a woman covering her head in the worship service by saying she should do this "on account of the angels." The meaning of the words is unmistakable, but what they refer to in this context is highly uncertain.

But where there is information implicit in the text itself, the translator may make it explicit in order to enable his readers to understand what the original readers easily understood. Contrary to what some might think, this does not add anything to the text; it simply gives the reader of the translation explicit information which was implicitly available to the original readers. It is obvious that this principle must be used with great care, and the translator must avoid the temptation to allow his cultural, doctrinal, and theological biases to influence his rendering of the original text.

To identify "Asia" in Acts 16:6 as a province is not to add any information to the text; it simply keeps the modern reader from taking the word to refer to the modern continent of Asia. Matthew 5:41 might not be accurately understood by the modern reader if translated literally, "If anyone forces you to go one mile, go with him two miles." The verb translated "forces" reflects the right which a Roman soldier in Palestine had of compelling a Jew to carry his pack one mile; this is made clear by translating, "And if one of the occupation troops forces you to carry his pack one mile, carry it another mile." Even such an apparently common and simple literary device as the use of the passive voice of the verb in order to avoid naming God as the actor must often be translated with a verb in the active voice, with God specified as the subject, in order to avoid giving the impression that the passive represents an impersonal subject. So in Matthew 5:7, "Blessed are the merciful, for they shall obtain mercy," is translated, "Happy are those who are merciful to others; God will be merciful to them." And Matthew 7:1-2 reads: "Do not judge others, so that God will not judge you—because God will judge you in the same way you judge others, and he will apply to you the same rules you apply to others."

The *New Testament in Today's English Version* has met with widespread approval and acceptance in the United States and abroad. It was given the Roman Catholic *imprimatur* by Richard Cardinal Cushing of Boston, with no changes in the text. But it has also been severely criticized on account of specific words and passages which differ in form from the more traditional versions.

The American Bible Society believes that there is room for different kinds of translations, aimed at different readers, and so it continues to publish and distribute various translations without attempting to dictate to anyone the choice of any particular translation as being superior to others. The Lord of the church is also the Lord of the Scriptures, and one can only rejoice over the fact that there is today an increasing use of the Scriptures, and that people everywhere are discovering anew, or for the first time, the message of the Bible for today.

Robert G. Bratcher
American Bible Society

The New English Bible

> We aim at a version which shall be as intelligible to contemporary readers as the original version was to its first readers—or as nearly so as possible. It is to be genuinely English in idiom . . . avoiding equally both archaisms and transient modernisms. The version should be plain enough to convey its meaning to any reasonably intelligent person . . . yet not bald or pedestrian. . . . It is to be hoped that, at least occasionally, it may produce arresting and memorable renderings. It should have sufficient dignity to be read aloud.

This statement by Dr. C. H. Dodd, General Director, Joint Committee, expresses the objectives of the sponsors and translators of *The New English Bible*, published in complete form on March 16, 1970, twenty-four years after the churches of Great Britain resolved that a new translation of the Bible be made in the language of the present day.

Meeting in October, 1946, representatives of the Church of England, the Church of Scotland, and the Methodist, Baptist, and Congregationalist Churches recommended that the work be a completely new translation, rather than a revision of any existing version. In 1947 they appointed a Joint Committee to carry the project to fruition, and in the following year invited other churches and Bible societies to participate. At a later date the hierarchies of the Roman Catholic Church of England and Scotland appointed observers. Recently two Roman Catholic scholars were named as full members of the Joint Committee.

What were the reasons for embarking on a new translation of the Bible? Evangelistic and educational motives were of major importance. Pastors, teachers, and youth leaders realized that the modern reader often failed to understand the beautiful and solemn, but frequently archaic, language of the classic English Bible, the King James Version. This hindered the church's work and witness.

There was general agreement that the English of the 1611 Bible is a fine literary medium; it contains noble and beautiful passages, both of prose and of poetry; it has influenced generations of later writers, and it has made the message of the Bible familiar to, and treasured by, generations of English-speaking Christians.

Nevertheless, the English language has changed so much that the King James Version no longer always conveys the correct meaning. The churches asked for a translation which would put the Bible message in language people could understand.

Recent developments in biblical scholarship were another significant concern. Much valuable work had been done, and many archaeological discoveries made during the past fifty years had fundamentally changed the interpretation of large parts of the Old Testament. All important manuscripts had been more thoroughly studied and compared. Older and more reliable manuscripts had been discovered. Knowledge of the biblical languages—Hebrew, Aramaic, and Greek—had been increased by the work of scholars using a wider range of sources and materials.

There was a strong feeling among the churches that the results of recent biblical scholarship should be made available to the general reader. Although a number of revisions of the Bible, as well as translations by individuals, had been made prior to 1946, it was felt that there should be a *new* translation, based on the most accurate and up-to-date findings (including the Dead Sea Scrolls) in all relevant fields of knowledge. It should be as truthful as human skill could make it, and should be carried out by the best scholars and translators that the churches possessed.

As the work began, one of the most important tasks of the Joint Committee was to appoint the translating panels charged, respectively, with the Old Testament, the New Testament, and the Apocrypha. Denominational considerations played no part in these appointments. In all cases the best qualified scholars in their respective subjects, from all universities, were enlisted.

Since what the Committee sought was a Bible combining the highest scholarly authority with a modern English style which would not put it at a disadvantage when set beside the classic English Bible, the King James Version, it also appointed a panel of Literary Advisers. This was composed of people who were not experts in the biblical languages but who were judged to have a strong sense of English style and to be sympathetic to the problems the translators would face, so that they could help the translators to find the best way of expressing their meaning in contemporary English.

Another important role of the Joint Committee was to provide guidance in determining how the objective, "that a translation of the Bible be made in the language of the present day," should be applied to the actual problems of Bible translation.

Certain principles were laid down:

> The work is to be a new translation . . . having as its object to render the original into contemporary English and avoiding all archaic words and forms of expression.
>
> Regard shall be paid to the native idiom and current usage of the English language, and Hebraisms and other un-English expressions shall be avoided; freedom shall be employed in altering the construction of the original where it is considered necessary to make the meaning intelligible in English.

A memorandum from the General Director, Dr. Dodd, pointed out that the new translation was intended for three classes of readers, who form "the public in view." The first was that large section of the population "which has no effective contact with the Church in any of its communions"; the second, those young people "for whom the Bible, if it is to make any impact, must be contemporary"; and finally, "intelligent people who do attend church, and for whom the traditional language is so familiar that its phrases slide over their minds almost without stirring a ripple."

Those responsible for *The New English Bible* resolved to issue it in a format which would reflect the high quality of the work itself, and which would be most helpful to the reader.

1. *Single-column Page.*—Because of the Bible's great length— more than 750,000 words—most Bibles are printed in double col-

umns of type. The Joint Committee decided to print the NEB in paragraph form in a single column on the page, with the poetry distinguished from the prose, and with the modern system of punctuation, so this translation in contemporary English would have the appearance of a contemporary book. (At a later date an edition with the text set in the traditional double-column format was issued by the British and Foreign Bible Society and by Cambridge University Press.)

2. *Verse Numbers.*—For more than 350 years the Bible has been printed in separate "verses," each numbered and beginning on a fresh line. This is a convenience rather than an intrinsic feature of the Bible. But because of the need to refer systematically to particular passages, some form of verse numbering is now essential; and this must be the traditional verse numbering to avoid making useless all existing commentaries, concordances, and other Bible study aids, and to make it easy to compare different versions. The NEB therefore retains the traditional verse numbers, but to avoid breaking the continuity of the text, they are placed in the margin.

In some cases, especially in the Old Testament, the translators' study of the text has convinced them that the original order has been disturbed in the manuscripts. They have restored what seems the most probable order of the text, and this may result in the verse numbers appearing out of numerical order. In a few cases (for example in Zechariah) it even results in the chapter numbers appearing out of order.

3. *Chapter Numbers and Headings Within Books.*—The traditional division of the Bible into chapters, which dates from the age of the later manuscripts, not from the original writings themselves, is not as a rule based on the major divisions of subject matter but on sections of approximately uniform length (a suitable length for one of the readings in a church service). Most major divisions of subject matter occupy several chapters, but less than a whole book.

In the NEB, chapter numbers, like verse numbers, have therefore been placed in the margin, and to give the modern reader the kind of guidance he might reasonably expect, each major division has been given a descriptive heading.

4. *Poetry.*—The Joint Committee's decision to print prose in paragraphs and poetry in verse form is in line with the practice of most modern translations, but the NEB alone also attempts to preserve the actual poetic structure of the Hebrew rhythms. In Hebrew, prose rises into poetry and poetry lapses into prose more easily than in modern languages, and there are passages which can be read as either. The NEB translators have followed their own judgment in doubtful cases.

5. *Footnotes.*—These are used in the NEB for several purposes, among them: to indicate where verses or parts of verses have been transposed, and to give alternative interpretations where the Hebrew is capable of such.

On March 14, 1961, the New Testament of *The New English Bible* was published jointly throughout the world by the Oxford and Cambridge University Presses. Since the Old Testament is about three times as long as the New and contains a greater variety of subject matter, it took much longer to finish this translation and to publish the complete Bible. The books known collectively as the Apocrypha were made available at the same time as the Old Testament, in March, 1970.

In summary, the final objective of *The New English Bible* is: to put into the hands of all kinds of persons, of whatever faiths, or none, a modern translation of the Bible that will be useful and understandable, and that at the same time will be rewarding and inspiring reading. The translators would not suggest that their work is perfect and that no further translation will ever need to be undertaken.

Nor does the NEB set itself up as a rival to the King James Version; the translators firmly believe that anyone who reads the NEB alongside the KJV will get a great deal more from the older version.

The NEB is intended to be, quite simply, the best that the best available scholars could produce, with the knowledge and evidence available to them. And they can claim, with complete assurance, that they have made sense of more obscure verses than any other translation and have solved many problems for the first time.

> The Editors
> Oxford University Press
> Cambridge University Press

New American Standard Bible 1971

The New Testament of the *New American Standard Bible* was produced and copyrighted by the Lockman Foundation in 1963. The whole Bible was released in 1971.

The *New American Standard Bible* was translated with the conviction that the words of Scripture as originally penned were inspired by God. Since they are the eternal words of God, the Holy Scriptures speak with fresh power to each generation, to give wisdom that leads to salvation, that men may serve God to the glory of Christ.

The translators had a twofold purpose in completing this translation: to adhere as closely as possible to the original languages of the Holy Scriptures, and to make the translation in a fluent and readable style according to current English usage. It required an aggregate total of nine years and seven months for the 58 scholars, expert in biblical languages, to complete the major task of researching and translating the many documents that resulted in the final text.

Because this translation follows the principles used in the translation of the American Standard Version of 1901 known as "the rock of biblical honesty," it is named the *New American Standard Bible.* It was completed in adherence to a four-fold aim, and as we glimpse these aims individually we can see why each is important.

The first aim was: "This translation shall be true to the original Hebrew and Greek." Dr. W. A. Criswell, noted Southern Baptist pastor, stated in *Why I Preach the Bible Is Literally True:* "There are those who speak of the inspiration of ideas as though the words were not particularly significant. They speak of the inspiration of ideas instead of the inspiration of words. But we cannot escape the equally vital significance of words. . . . The self-disclosure and the revelation was made in words. It was not in the general realm of ideas. . . . We cannot have melody without music or mathematics without numbers. Neither can we have a divine record of God without words, and if that divine record is to be a true revelation of God, it must be without error. It must be infallibly correct."

A formal equivalence test, which discovers how close a Bible translation is to the original words of Holy Scripture, was recently completed. Those Bibles tested included the most popular modern Bibles. This test indicated that the *New American Standard Bible,* as a word-by-word translation, deviates less from the original languages than any other modern Bible tested.

The second aim that guided the translation process was: "It shall be grammatically correct." Many hours were spent in rendering the grammar and terminology in contemporary English. When it was felt that the word-for-word literalness of the translation was unacceptable to the modern reader, a change was made in the direction of a more current English idiom. In these instances, the more literal rendering has been preserved in the margin.

Words are the vehicle of thought, and most languages, especially the English, have a flexibility which economic and cultural progress utilizes. Passing time, with myriads of inventions and innovations, automatically renders obsolete and inexpressive many words that once were in acceptable usage.

The ever-present danger of stripping divine truth of its dignity and original intent was prominently before the minds of the producers at all times. The editorial board therefore was staffed with Greek and Hebrew scholars as well as leading pastors of Bible-believing churches.

The third aim that guided the translators was: "It shall be understandable to the masses." To make God's original revelation understandable to the masses, the translators used marginal readings. In addition to the more literal renderings, the marginal notations have been made to include alternate translations, readings of variant manuscripts, and explanatory equivalents of the text. Only such notations have been used as have been felt justified in assisting the reader's comprehension of the terms used by the original Author. The enthusiastic response of the general public to the *New American Standard Bible* bespeaks the value of this care in making the translation understandable.

The fourth of the four-fold aim was: "This translation shall give the Lord Jesus Christ His proper place, the place which the Word gives Him; no work will ever be personalized." This aim adheres to the goal stated in Colossians 1:18, "so that He Himself (speaking of Christ) might come to have first place in everything."

F. Dewey Lockman, founder of the Lockman Foundation, believed that God made funds available through the claiming of God's promise in Malachi 3:10, " 'Bring the whole tithe into the storehouse, so that there may be food in My house, and test Me now in this,' says the LORD of hosts, 'if I will not open for you the windows of heaven, and pour out for you a blessing until there is no more need.' " Mr. Lockman believed that all any of us have to offer to God is our own availability. He believed that God made all of the $850,000 available for the major purpose of translating his Word. He often regretted that United States copyright laws make it mandatory for the producer's name to appear on the translation, because he most definitely believed that only Christ should be glorified by the translation of God's Holy Word.

Because of the fourth aim none of the 58 outstanding Christian scholars who worked on this monumental task have affixed their signatures to their work. If they had, there would be recognized some of the finest Greek and Hebrew New Testament and Old Testament scholars.

Dr. Criswell has written very explicitly to this point when he stated in the book mentioned above: "When we open the Scriptures, we find that sometimes the penman is Moses, sometimes it is Daniel, sometimes . . . John, or Paul. But did these men claim to be the authors of the Bible? Did they compose this tremendous Volume? Do they divide the honors among themselves? No! For this Volume is the writing of the Living God."

This four-fold aim was adopted in the beginning of this translation because the Board of the Lockman Foundation was impressed by the Holy Spirit that this was the direction to take. Each of the scholars who worked on this translation was led by the Holy Spirit to accept this responsibility of translation, and they voluntarily adopted the four-fold aim as the guide for their work. These men met in plenary sessions and prayerfully, under the leadership of God's Holy Spirit did the work God had placed before them. No interpretation was ever made by any one single person.

Among those who have been blessed by this translation are the following:

Harold L. Fickett, Jr., pastor, First Baptist Church, Van Nuys, California: "I am convinced that this translation is the most accurate of any on the market today. It is a must in the library of one who is meticulous in the study of the Word of God."

A world-renowned Bible teacher and author, Dr. Wilbur M. Smith: "In my opinion this is certainly the most accurate and the most revealing translation . . . that we now have. I intend to keep it on my desk for immediate access during the years that remain to me."

Duke K. McCall, president, Southern Baptist Theological Seminary, Louisville, Kentucky: "Because of the integrity with which the Hebrew and Greek text was translated, this new edition retains the great value of the original, literal translation. The changes made appear to retain accuracy while facilitating reading and understanding. This is a valuable new tool for a Bible student whose conviction of the inspiration of Scripture produces concern for precisely accurate translation of Hebrew and Greek text."

S. H. Sutherland, president
The Lockman Foundation

The Living Bible, Paraphrased

The following paragraphs are from the preface of this work and are adapted from the preface to the first edition of *Living Letters*.

This book, though arriving late on the current translation scene, has been under way for many years. It has undergone several major manuscript revisions and has been under the careful scrutiny of a team of Greek and Hebrew experts to check content, and of English critics for style. Their many suggestions have been largely followed, though none of those consulted feels entirely satisfied with the present result. There is therefore a tentative edition. Further suggestions as to both renderings and style will be gladly considered as future printings are called for.

A word should be said here about paraphrases. What are they? To paraphrase is to say something in different words than the author used. It is a restatement of an author's thoughts, using different words than he did. This book is a paraphrase of the Old and New Testaments. Its purpose is to say as exactly as possible what the writers of the Scriptures meant, and to say it simply, expanding where necessary for a clear understanding by the modern reader.

The Bible writers often used idioms and patterns of thought that are hard for us to follow today. Frequently the thought sequence is fast-moving, leaving gaps for the reader to understand and fill in, or the thought jumps ahead or backs up to something said before (as one would do in conversation) without clearly stating the antecedent reference. . . .

Then too, the writers often have compressed enormous thoughts into single technical words that are full of meaning, but need expansion and amplification if we are to be sure of understanding what the author meant to include in such words as "justification," "righteousness," "redemption," "baptism for the dead," "elect," and "saints." Such amplification is permitted in a paraphrase but exceeds the responsibilities of a strict translation.

There are dangers in paraphrases, as well as values. For whenever the author's exact words are not translated from the original languages, there is a possibility that the translator, however honest, may be giving the English reader something that the original writer did not mean to say. This is because a paraphrase is guided not only by the translator's skill in simplifying but also by the clarity of his understanding of what the author meant and by his theology. For when the Greek or Hebrew is not clear, then the theology of the translation is his guide, along with his sense of logic, unless perchance the translation is allowed to stand without any clear meaning at all. The theological lodestar in this book has been a rigid evangelical position.

The following is a review of this book by Dr. Marv Mayers of Wheaton College and was supplied by Tyndale House Publishers for the present use.

For decades and centuries the Christian has attempted to get others (his children, unbelievers, etc.) to read the Bible. Tyndale House, under the direction of Ken Taylor, has instead *made the Bible readable.* Besides the content being immediately understandable by the average person, the format in which it is presented has taken on a new look of elegance. The volume has "presence." It is giftable in a new way: readability and appearance.

The volume has much greater significance than this, however, for it represents significant advances in the area of translation theory. With the King James Version of the Bible, "everyone" was forced to *be his own translator,* once the specific dialect of English spoken in King James's day ceased to be spoken by the common man. This has resulted in various falsehoods being perpetuated in the Christian church. The average Christian living today is not trained to be a translator. He lacks the knowledge of the original languages; he lacks training in linguistic principles, and he is unaware of approaches and tools to use with cross-cultural nuance—let alone knowing that such nuance exists. Those Bible readers and students recognizing their lack of training in translation called upon the Bible scholar to translate and interpret the King James Version for them, and they furiously recorded these gems of "truth" in notebooks or in the margins of their Bibles so that when they read that passage again they can understand it.

Thus, with the introduction of *The Living Bible* and other such popular or "vulgate" versions, the average middle class American Christian could read the Bible for himself, interpret it automatically in keeping with his historical and cultural backgrounds, and let the Holy Spirit direct his understanding in an individual and personal way. A vulgate translation lets *everyman be priest* in Calvin's sense of the word.

Though Tyndale House terms their latest version of the Bible a "paraphrase," it is in reality a vulgate translation in the specific dialect of a language group or subculture. *The Living Bible* has become a *model for translations* throughout the world where Bible translators are striving to present the Bible in the language of the members of specific ethnic-linguistic groups. This does not negate the value of other translations. It simply says every subculture needs its own translation.

Perhaps the most significant contribution of *The Living Bible* to translation theory lies in its being an *impact translation*. In former years of translation development, the word-for-word or "literal" translation was in vogue. This close adherence to the very words of Scripture seemed to be the only way truth could be maintained and perpetuated. Every word had an "absolute" quality or meaning and could only be utilized to signify that which the word intended. In languages where there did not seem to be a word for *love* or *sin,* or where the impression was gained that this was not the same quality of love or sin as we understood it, a "loan" word would be used that was foreign to the language but not foreign to the literal translator. In English, a version without "virgin" or "blood" was inaccurate, and thus heretical. Translation theory progressed to a stage of "concept" translation, or the translating of idea to idea or concept to concept rather than word for word. This permitted translators to expand the word usage to get closer to the range of meaning intended in the original usage.

An impact translation is one that permits the reader to respond in the full way the original hearer-reader responded, that lets the

Word of God resonate in his entire life being. He laughs hilariously with the participant who has experienced the miracle of deliverance from some great trial (Judges 5). He weeps deeply and contritely with the Hebrew weeping because he sensed he so often played the "fool" (Numbers 11:11-15). But more, as he reads, he gets caught up in the total argument of Scripture that has its "answer" and fulfillment in Christ. He cannot help but focus on Christ and open his life to him since he has become totally involved. The literal translation focusing on the Word as words, the concept translation focusing on the Word as idea-concepts, fall short of an impact translation focusing on the Word as *living Christ*.

Besides making contributions in the area of translation theory, *The Living Bible* confronts us as a tremendous *tool of evangelism*. . . . A person receiving *The Living Bible* expects neither to understand it nor to like it, in keeping with his past experience with more obscure translations. He begins reading and finds it so readable he begins to like what he reads and winds up "converting" to that which he reads. Thus he does not have to learn a language before he can respond to God. Therefore, as a counter pressure, used wisely under the guidance of the Spirit of God, the Bible can once again be used as a tool of mass evangelism—a function primarily filled now, not by the Bible, but by the evangelist. . . .

The Living Bible will be an exciting, lived experience for those who are unfamiliar with "holy" language, those who enjoy being "priests" to God, those who grow personally in their spiritual lives while opening the Word privately or in the small group and asking the question, "What does God's Word say to me?"

The question today, more than ever before, is: What is the point of the Bible? Is it a book for scholars? Is it a book for the "elites" in Christianity? Is it a book simply for study in the formal sense of "classroom" study? Or is it a book for people—a book for people hungering for the meaning and purpose of life—a book that will open to every man the exciting, living Christ?

The New International Bible: New Testament 1973

Long before the present flurry of new English translations of the Bible, *The New International Version* had its beginnings. Back in the middle fifties, theologians who had a high view of Scripture explored the desirability and feasibility of a modern translation. Opinions were garnered from men of wide and diverse theological and denominational backgrounds. The consensus was that, in spite of the fine features of many translations, there was a need for an up-to-date translation that was faithful to the original language. Guidelines were formed and committees established, and in 1967, under the sponsorship of the New York Bible Society International (established in 1809), the actual work of the translation was launched.

A governing committee of fifteen—made up of theologians from different American colleges, universities, and theological seminaries—was established. Dr. Edwin H. Palmer, a former pastor in the Christian Reformed Church and professor of systematic theology at Westminster Theological Seminary, was chosen to be the Executive Secretary.

Over a hundred scholars—in Old Testament, New Testament, systematic theology, and English sytle—were selected to contribute to the translation. They represented a great number of denominations, such as the Baptist, Brethren, Church of Christ, Episcopal, Lutheran, Mennonite, Methodist, Nazarene, Presbyterian, and Reformed. Such a wide representation of so many different denominations and theological backgrounds has kept the NIV from a provincial, sectarian bias, making it transdenominational in character.

Not only does it cut across denominations at times, but also across the English-speaking nations. Men from the United States, Great Britain, New Zealand, Canada, and Australia have worked on it, giving it an international scope. Although a Commonwealth edition was published—one that would avoid American spellings and idioms—it is remarkable how few changes in wording had to be adopted for it. The NIV does have an international style, one that does not jar the ear of the Englishman, Australian, or American.

The working procedures also gave the NIV a distinctive character. Each book of the Bible was assigned to a team of scholars, some of whom had made that book their specialty either by teaching courses in it or writing a commentary on it. This team produced the first draft of the translation of that book. Next, an Intermediate Editorial Committee of at least five men went over the team translation, with constant reference to the Hebrew, Aramaic, and Greek. Their work then went to a General Editorial Committee, which rechecked it in relation to the original languages and made another thorough revision. Both the Intermediate and General Editorial Committees were composed of no fewer than five men—men who had often worked at a prior level of translation. This cross-fertilization helped to keep a unity of style.

Finally, the product of the General Editorial Committee went to the top committee of fifteen, which had the final responsibility of presenting to the New York Bible Society International an acceptable translation. They, too, went over every translation word by word, checking for accuracy, clarity, idiom, uniformity of style, and dignity.

Before and after the revision by the top committee, English stylists were called in to review meticulously the tentative translations. The translations were also sent out to the many editors and translators, as well as to various other people—young and old, educated and uneducated, ministers and laymen—to be tested for clarity and idiom.

This whole translation process was long and costly. But it helped to produce a mature translation, free from the idiosyncrasies of a single translator or small group of translators, and free from sectarian bias. Regardless of how good an individual translator may be, he has blind spots, foibles, and limited abilities. The risks involved in these problems can be safeguarded by having many pairs of eyes reviewing the same product.

The goals of the translators were fourfold:

1. *Accuracy.* Since all the translators had to subscribe to the belief in the inspiration and infallibility of the Bible, they desired to produce a translation that reflects precisely what God has written through the prophets and apostles. They are adverse to paraphrases and loose translations.

2. *Clarity.* Many people brought up on the King James Version believe they understand it. But the fact is that the archaic words and outmoded sentence structure seriously hamper most laymen— even though they do not realize it—from adequately understanding the rich truths of God's Word. Repeatedly, even the translators, who thought they knew what the Bible said, found that as they tried to put the original into modern English, they did not truly understand it either. And they were forced to translate in a new way so that the meaning of the original could be brought out clearly. However, this did not mean that they were at liberty to water down or alter hard-to-understand biblical truths. Those passages that had innately difficult ideas had to be left as difficult in English as they were in the Hebrew or Greek.

3. *Contemporary idiom.* The one question that was constantly asked during the translation process was: "But how would you say it today?" Again and again scholars, steeped in and mesmerized by the King James, tended to reproduce phrases that seemed natural to them because they had heard and read them so often. For example, the King James says, "Man shall not live by bread alone" (Matt. 4:4). The NIV translated it "on bread alone." Most people, reared on the King James will ask: "Why change it? 'By' sounds so natural." Yes, it sounds natural if you have heard that proverb all your life in the King James language. But the question is: "How would you say it today?" Who would say that Japanese

live "by fish," or Chinese "by rice"? Nobody, for the idiom is "on," not "by." So the question was asked repeatedly: "Is it idiomatic?" And because of the hypnosis the King James holds over most biblical scholars, it was necessary to have many scholars, stylists, and laymen tell the translators what sounded natural or what sounded strained to their ear.

4. *Dignity.* It would be possible for a translation to have these three characteristics and yet to lack dignity or to be coarse in expression. But one goal of the translators was to have a translation suitable, not only for private use, but also for public worship. They wanted one that has dignity without being stuffy, one that is so beautiful, clear, and accurate that a person would want to memorize from it. Calvin Linton, professor of English literature and dean of arts and sciences at George Washington University, expressed it when he said: "High on the list of stylistic characteristics of the NIV is a kind of economical integrity, a quality of simple dignity, of tightly drawn texture, 'wov'n close, both matter, form and stile,' to quote Milton in another connection. Here is no straining after catchy colloquialism, shirt-sleeve casualness, or perky slang."

An unintentional but noteworthy by-product of the working procedures and goals of the NIV is its familiarity together with freshness. As one reads it, he feels at home and not jarred by unusual expressions. There is a freshness to the translation, and yet "the comfort of a tested friendship" (Linton). If 1 Corinthians 13 or John 3 or John 14 are read apart from the King James, one will feel at home with it. Yet, if he will carefully compare these passages with the King James, he will find many improvements.

Dale Miller, chairman of the religion department at Drake University, writes that the NIV "is a solid, sound translation in very readable English and could well replace the Revised Standard as the best English Bible now available." Whether that prediction will be true or not only time will tell. Even though the Old Testament is not finished, several denominations are studying the NIV

New Testament carefully for possible adoption. The Old Testament is scheduled to go to press in 1978.

Edwin H. Palmer, Executive Secretary
New International Version
New York Bible Society International

4. The Bibles We Like and Use

Dr. Jimmy R. Allen, pastor, First Baptist Church, San Antonio, Texas, writes:

Those of us schooled in the magnificent sounds of Elizabethan language in the King James Version of the Bible find ourselves continuing to use it as a basic text. I preach from the King James Version regularly. It is in the pews of our church meeting place. We read it together each Sunday. Its limitations are many, but it is still a moving and meaningful experience for the hundreds of people gathering for worship to read from the text used for centuries by English-speaking Christians.

I do not hesitate, however, to utilize the modern English versions, both in study and in sermonic material. My personal favorite source of devotional reading is *The New Testament in Modern English* by J. B. Phillips. While occasionally I feel other translations are superior, the moving way in which he captures the spirit of the New Testament in the English language never fails to grip my imagination.

When I want to verify the accuracy of a translation in contemporary English, I use the *New English Bible*. In my judgment it is the most accurate treatment of the Bible available in English. I use it regularly in my study.

The New Testament in *The Living Bible* is a paraphrase, but it is a useful tool. It makes the Bible come alive for young people and adults alike. Not only do I keep this New Testament available for my own reading, but I give it away from a supply in my office. I give it to searchers for whom the Bible is a mysterious and difficult-to-comprehend book and also to new Christians. I carefully explain its paraphrase nature, but I am thankful that Kenneth Taylor has been used of God to make the Scriptures come to life in such a beautiful way. In similar fashion I use *Today's English Version*. Although more accurate than *The Living Bible*, it lacks the flow of lively descriptions of Ken Taylor's work.

To the criticism by some that these varying versions lack accuracy in one place or another, my response is that nothing that is essential to understanding how to meet God and what he promises to do in our life has been left out. Something that is very essential has been included. It is the reverent listening spirit of serious people who are seeking to discern the mind of God and to follow his commands. There is a great danger in making the Bible an end in itself, but it is an instrument. It is a tool. It is a road map. It has authority . . . because it is the record of God's revelation. There was a time when I was more intrigued with the words that I was memorizing and quoting than I was listening and doing. There are some people who are so interested in memorizing road maps that they do not take the journey. God speaks to us through the instructions on the road map in order to get us to follow the road and to experience the presence of his Spirit in our journey.

DR. HAROLD C. BENNETT, executive secretary-treasurer, Florida Baptist Convention, Jacksonville, writes:

This is a personal testimony of what the Bible means to me for I believe "the word of our God shall stand forever" (Isa. 40:8). I feel the Bible is God's message to me, and that it can become God's message through me to others.

As a denominational minister, it is my privilege to preach in many churches. In the pulpit I usually read the text of the sermon from the King James Version. The congregation responds best when

I read a passage meaningfully and with expression. However, occasionally I will read the passage from one of the other fine translations or even from a paraphrase of the Bible. I identify the version carefully.

When studying the Bible, I use the King James Version and then compare it with other translations. The *Revised Standard Version* is a helpful translation. I also use the *American Standard Version, The Amplified Bible,* and *Today's English Version.* These help me to understand Scripture passages better and to relate their meaning more effectively to life today.

For devotional Bible reading, I use a variety of translations. Although the King James Version is the standby, I read with benefit and inspiration *Today's English Version* and *The Living New Testament.*

When I have taken time to read and understand the Word of God, I have found that I can trust it completely.

DR. BENJAMIN R. BRUNER, pastor, First Baptist Church, Cumberland, Maryland, writes:

When visiting the elderly and shut-ins, I use the King James Version most of the time. I find the comforting passages are more familiar and helpful to them in that translation. Convenience may influence my decision for I have found pocket-size New Testament and Psalms carried in an inside pocket of my coat the easiest and least conspicuous way of having with me at all times a copy of the New Testament. I have not found a convenient pocket-size in other translations. For the non-churched, I formerly used the *Revised Standard Version* since it is close kin to the King James but often clearer. When *Today's English Version* came out, I started using it for them. I find they grasp it better than any other translation.

Until the *New English Bible* came out, I preferred *The New Testament in Modern Speech* by Weymouth above all others for personal devotions because it seemed clear excellent English and translated the Greek idioms smoothly. Since the *New English Bible* comes closer to combining stately beauty as literature and accuracy of translation than any translation I have seen, I now use it.

For devotional study I start each quarter of the year reading one chapter of the Gospels a day in one of several modern translations. I continue reading that translation a chapter a day until I have completed the New Testament, I use some of the older ones, such as Moffatt, Twentieth Century, Goodspeed, Montgomery, Williams, but I also use some of the more recent, such as the *Today's English Version,* Barclay, *Living Bible,* or *New American Standard Bible.* I find each makes its distinctive contribution to my understanding. As to the Old Testament, I read through in a modern translation with a chapter from the Pentateuch and one from history, one from the Writings and one from the Prophets at a sitting. Gradually, therefore, I complete reading the entire Old Testament in all of the more than a dozen modern translations I have, from the Improved Edition to *New American Standard Bible.* My favorite versions of the Old Testament are *Revised Standard Version* and *The New English Bible.*

In my sermonic preparation I use almost every translation I have, selecting that which seems to me to best fit my understanding of the Hebrew and the Greek.

I find the *Amplified Bible* and the Expanded New Testament helpful in study but almost never use them in public reading because they are too clumsy.

In the pulpit I use whatever translation, modern or older, I think most nearly fits in with what I believe is the meaning of the passage.

For funerals I most often use the King James because of its familiarity to many people. Frequently I read passages from the *Revised Standard Version* and occasionally from *The New English Bible.* I may find in them the twist of experience that seems nearest to helping the bereaved. I rarely use other translations for funerals.

Sometimes I identify what translation I am using and sometimes

I do not, depending upon my own feeling and sense of need at the moment.

DR. T. T. CRABTREE, pastor, First Baptist Church, Springfield Missouri, writes:

Beginning the first of last January, 1974, I began using the *Revised Standard Version* as my pulpit Bible. I do this all of the time unless I should use some other version like Phillips or *The New English Bible.*

I became convinced one day while listening to an associate read the Scriptures for the morning message in the King James Version that in many instances the King James Version conceals the meaning rather than reveals the meaning. At least at the point of conveying the full thought of what the inspired writer was trying to communicate. I decided then that I would change to a modern version.

I decided on using the *Revised Standard Version,* which had been my study Bible for a number of years, after listening to an evaluation of all of the modern versions on a cassette tape. It was the conclusion of scholars and pastors across the country that the best version now available is the *Revised Standard Version.*

Thus far I have had no complaints, at least not to me personally, from any of my congregation for this change to the *Revised Standard Version.* I have had a number of favorable comments. I am confident that a few of the folk wish that I was using the King James Version.

I believe that *The Living Bible* is probably the version or paraphrase which is most popular in our congregation other than the King James Version. I have found it to be very good at times and have used it on several occasions.

DR. WALTER R. DAVIS, pastor, East Dayton Baptist Church, Dayton, Ohio, Writes:

I use the King James translation of the Bible in the pulpit and for memorization. I like the beautiful flow of the English language as well as the dramatic way the words are placed in poetic style.

One of my favorite sermon preparation sources is *The New Testament: an Expanded Translation* by Kenneth A. Wuest.

I use the Greek New Testament also for study and sermon building, as well as seed planting for future messages to be delivered.

During our Bible study and devotions at home, I lead the family in a time of worship with King James, and for clarification, reference is made to the *Living Bible*. For my own personal devotion time I enjoy the use of *The American Translation of the New Testament* by E. J. Goodspeed.

In researching various texts, I use the *New English Bible* and for a super amplification of texts I use *Letters to Young Churches* by J. B. Phillips. Another translation I enjoy using is *The New Testament in Four Versions*.

When reading the Bible in worship, occasionally I insert a free translation from the original Greek to give a better understanding of the Scriptures.

DR. WAYNE DEHONEY, pastor, Walnut Street Baptist Church, Louisville, Kentucky, writes:

I use a number of translations and paraphrases as well as commentaries on the Greek text in the course of my Bible study, sermon preparation, and public reading of the Scripture. It depends upon the purpose of my reading as to which I use and find most meaningful.

For my own personal devotional reading I prefer one of the modern paraphrases, first choice being *The Living Bible*. Second choice is *Today's English Version*. I seldom read the King James for my own personal devotional life.

Out of the devotional readings come phrases, concepts in the language of today, etc., that give me sermon ideas and suggestions for further development. I find these paraphrases, plus Phillips and Moffatt, as very helpful in giving me a sermon idea, a sermon topic or title, or a fresh approach to a familiar passage of Scripture.

In my indepth study, I do not rely upon contemporary translations but go back to commentaries that assist me in exploring the meaning of the original Greek or Hebrew. I will sometimes go from these to word studies in the original language. It is in this study that I check out the doctrinal soundness of the paraphrase that I might be using in the sermon.

In the public reading of the Scripture in the worship service, I frequently use the *Living Bible* and *Today's English Version* for power to communicate the central thoughts of the passage to the congregation. I am not greatly concerned about the finer points of translation that may give a different shade of meaning to certain sections of the passage for I want to communicate clear understandable concepts to the congregation in this public reading. However, I use the King James Version for the familiar passages—such as 1 Corinthians 13, the 23rd Psalm, etc. There is a certain grandeur about the King James from a literary viewpoint, and if the passage is familiar, there is value in recalling these preconceived associations.

I am well aware of some points of contention in various paraphrases and new translations that have some validity. I would not use these passages in public—but I see no reason for not using other passages that are accurately translated and express the concepts with such clarity and understanding in the language of the day. When you have fish, you eat the meat and spit out the bones!

DR. RUSSELL DILDAY, pastor, Second-Ponce de Leon Baptist
Church, Atlanta, Georgia, writes:

The translation of the Bible which I use most of the time is
the King James Version. I use it for the same reasons a golfer
stays with his old wooden-shafted putter. It feels comfortable to
him and has always served his needs very well. This is the way
I feel about the King James translation. It has its limitations and
because of language long since outdated, its meanings are not
always very clear. However, when verses long familiar and often
memorized are shared together in a worship service in the King
James wording, there seems to be an immediate feeling of iden-
tification on the part of the congregation. This familiar translation
creates a feeling of mutuality that brings the congregation together.
If it were necessary to give up every other translation of the Scriptures but one, for me that one would be the King James Version.

However, from time to time in order to bring out with greater
clarity and emphasis or meaning in a particular passage, other
translations are helpful. I like the *Revised Standard Version* because
of its punctuation and paragraph arrangement. Very often the
over-all meaning of an extended passage is lost by the chapter
and verse divisions in the King James. The RSV is an improvement
over the King James in this regard. I like the *New Testament in
Modern Speech* by Phillips for its accuracy and its clarity of meaning. *The Living Bible,* while it is a paraphrase and not a translation,
is very valuable in presenting time-worn biblical truths in fresh,
attention-getting language. Very often a passage which is easily
taken for granted because of familiarity can come alive with new
understanding when shared in the paraphrased form. A caution
here is necessary, however, in the very nature of a paraphrase.
The passage one intends to use must be carefully checked for
accuracy of meaning against another translation or the Greek text
itself. If the original meaning has not been distorted, then *The
Living Bible* paraphrase is often a helpful asset.

DR. CHARLES G. FULLER, pastor, First Baptist Church, Roanoke, Virginia, writes:

The two translations I find most appealing and helpful in worship services are the King James Version and *The Living Bible, Paraphrased.* The King James translation seems to help worshipers identify with a continuing legacy while *The Living Bible* provides a freshness and sense of currency about the message of God.

For my own devotional reading I am finding myself more and more drawn to *The Living Bible.* Reading that particular paraphrase allows me the benefit of relaxation at the point of comprehension so that I am able to concentrate upon personal application. It seems to me that for devotional reading of the Scriptures one is best served by a feeling of intimacy. For that reason, as well, I enjoy *The Living Bible.*

Though I would make no pretense about my abilities in using the Greek New Testament, I do attempt to use it in my sermon study. Such a practice not only keeps me updated with a fair ability to use the Greek, but it also enhances a sense of authenticity in preaching.

The King James Version, *The Living Bible, The New Testament in Modern English* by Phillips, and *The Expanded Translation* by Wuest are all translations to which I regularly turn in study.

With respect to word studies in the Old Testament I find the American Standard Version is quite adequate and most helpful.

In my opinion, some of the most graphic word renderings are to be found in Phillips' *New Testament in Modern English.* As for the most helpful version when trying to transfer biblical thought to the modern mind-set, there can be little question that *The Living Bible* is without equal.

Due to the continued use of the King James Version and *The Living Bible* in our worship services, we find that our congregation responds to both and for the reasons mentioned previously. As most churches, however, ours still finds a reverence for the King

James Version, which will continue for time to come.

Dr. David R. Grant, pastor, Broadmoor Baptist Church, Jackson, Mississippi, writes:

Most of the time I use the King James Version of the Bible. There are several reasons for this. One is because I am more used to it. Verses I memorized early in life came from this translation and are, therefore, more familiar to me. Another reason is that most of the Bible helps that I have, such as concordances, reference books, etc., are based on this translation and consequently, it is easier to use. This is also true in regard to the people who hear me preach. Although I have studied Hebrew and Greek and have a number of other translations available, I still believe the King James Version is an accurate translation. In fact, in my opinion, it is about as accurate as one can find.

Still another reason I use the King James Version is because of the beauty of it. This may not be a scholarly reason, but it certainly is an aesthetic one.

I do use the *Revised Standard Version* a great deal in my study because I believe it to be an accurate translation and also because its contemporary language helps me understand the Scriptures. I also find that many of the later commentaries and helps are based on this particular translation.

Beyond this, I use many of the modern translations for variations and for understanding. My use here is primarily for personal devotions, but at times I do read them from the pulpit because some of these versions are interpretations and not just translations.

Dr. Elmer L. Gray, editor, *The California Southern Baptist*, Fresno, California, writes:

The Bible is an essential reference book for the Christian writer. I write items that range from editorials and news stories to articles and curriculum materials. Therefore, I keep several translations close at hand as I write.

The translation I use most is the King James Version. I use it because the readers of what I write are better acquainted with it than with any other single translation. I use it to check references from the concordance, to make sure of precise wording, and to discover basically the content of a passage.

I depend on other translations then to sharpen my understanding of biblical content. My next most used translation is the *Revised Standard Version* which I read in addition to the KJV almost every time I refer to a passage. Often the RSV will clarify phrases or words that are difficult to understand in the KJV. The King James uses words and phrases in ways that were common several hundred years ago but not common today. At times its meaning is hard to make out but much clearer in the *Revised Standard Version*.

Besides these I use some of the more modern versions like I would a commentary. I read them realizing that the translators or paraphrasers have taken some liberties with the original language in order to express their understanding of the meaning in current speech. I find *The New English Bible, The Living Bible,* and *Today's English Version* helpful when I am trying to explain the meaning of a Scripture passage. After reading the passage in the KJV and RSV, I read it again in one or two of the modern speech versions, and then I have a clear enough idea of the meaning of the passage to express it in my own words.

REV. WOODROW W. HILL, assistant editor, *Biblical Recorder,* Raleigh, North Carolina, writes:

Many people have cut their spiritual teeth on the King James Version, and it seems almost a sacrilege to them to read any other version. They rightly find a halo of authority associated with it which seems strangely absent when they read a modern translation. No one should interfere with their respect for this venerated version, and neither should they disparage those who find more relevance in others.

The language of the King James is elevated and classical, and these qualities generate awe and inspire worship in one who has practiced a long time reverence for it. There is much to be said for this, and some will never find the same satisfaction in reading other translations.

In addition to personal study of the King James, there are those who find a nostalgia associated with it which carries them back to mother's knee, and to family devotions conducted by the father in the home. Recollections of pulpit readings from it in childhood years add to the nostalgia. Also, most who possess this quality of reverence for the King James have involved themselves in memorizing the more familiar passages in the Bible, and it seems almost as though violence has been done to those verses when everyday langauge is employed in communicating such sacred truths. The Beatitudes, the Lord's Prayer, the Sermon on the Mount, and the Ten Commandments can never be quite the same in the mundane language of today to those who possess this kind of awe for the 1611 version.

Fault must not be found with these people who seemingly represent a passing generation. To the contrary, they may be communicating a lesson in reverence for the Word of God badly needed by today's children, who may be more enlightened but less reverent. When knowledge and respect are weighed against each other in dealing with sacred things, it seems indisputable that respect should come out on top.

While the original language of the New Testament was conversational in nature, the truths communicated were elevated and spiritual. For this reason it seems inappropriate to many for the vehicle used in conveying these sacred truths to have too much of the smell of the mundane upon it.

This in no way diminishes the value of versions couched in simpler and more modern language. The primer has always served a purpose, but one who grows in language and spirit is able to make the transition to more elevated levels. Those who began with King James did not start with the easiest version to understand.

The real test of any translation lies in that which occurs in its readers. If it proves to be an instrument leading them to a better understanding of God and their relation to him, its divine purpose has been accomplished. Let critics beware lest they find themselves fighting against God.

DR. JOE L. INGRAM, executive secretary, Baptist General Convention of Oklahoma, Oklahoma City, writes:

It is rather difficult to say which translation of the Bible I like best. Usually I use the King James Version in the pulpit because I feel that most people in the congregation are more familiar with it than with other versions.

Several years ago I started reading the Bible through each year in a different version: American Standard Version, Smith-Goodspeed, *The New English Bible, Revised Standard Version, The Amplified Bible, New American Standard Bible,* and *The Living Bible, a Paraphrase.* I have spent more time with New Testament translations. In studying a passage of Scripture, I usually compare several versions.

I am especially fond of William Barclay's two-volume *The New Testament.* For me he captures the biblical words, manners, and customs in his translation without making it read like a commentary. I like to read a "book" at a time just for sheer spiritual enjoyment. I have found that most of my sermon ideas come from "the overflow" of such reading than from studying for a sermon. Barclay fires my imagination.

Also, I am very fond of *The New International Version.* When it comes out in a more usable form, I will probably use it from the pulpit. It combines the beauty of the King James with the accuracy of the American Standard. The translators have recognized the worldwide character of the English language and have avoided both Americanisms and Anglicisms. The more I read it, the more I feel it is becoming an "anchor" translation for me.

I also make extensive use of *The New Testament in the Language of the People* by Charles B. Williams. I have been using it regularly for twenty years. It avoids paraphrase and adheres faithfully to the Greek. Dr. Williams made his greatest contribution in revealing the tense distinctions in the Greek verbs.

DR. L. D. JOHNSON, chaplain, Furman University, Greenville, South Carolina, writes:

In response to your request for a statement on what Bible I use, I will offer the following:

I do not use any translation exclusively, because I regard all translations as the efforts of devout men to capture the essence of biblical truth and express it in a language foreign to the writers. One translation may be clearer at one place and another at another place.

For the most part, I use the *Revised Standard Version* in teaching. On the whole I consider it to be an accurate translation of the Bible. I suspect I use it most commonly because I know it best, having worked with it since it was published. I have notes on probably 90% of the *Revised Standard* text of the Bible. Obviously, these are valuable to me.

However, I do not use the RSV without checking other translations and frequently check the Hebrew or Greek text as well. Other translations I value include *The New English Bible* and *The Jerusalem Bible.*

I suspect that on the whole *The New English Bible* comes nearer to translating accurately the sense of the original text than any other translation in our possession. However, I find that some of its expressions are unfamiliar to our American idiom. I do not think it reads as smoothly as the RSV to an American.

I like *The Jerusalem Bible* for its freshness and for the different slant it gives on certain ideas. I consider it a very good translation.

I also read numerous other translations done either by individuals or committees. Among these are the Moffatt translation, *The New Testament in Modern English* by Phillips, *Today's English Version,* and the *New American Bible* published by the Catholic Biblical Association of America.

However, to repeat, for classroom use I prefer the Oxford Annotated edition of the RSV.

DR. E. EARL JOINER, professor of religion, Stetson University, DeLand, Florida, writes:

Like millions of others in the English-speaking world, I was brought up on the King James Version of the Bible and do not remember being told or asking if there was any other. In fact it was not until I entered college that I first learned that there were other translations, and I consider it fortunate in retrospect that, as a college freshman, in the same year I became acquainted with the American Standard Version (1901 Revision), I was also introduced to the study of the Greek New Testament, and to a scholarly approach to biblical study. All of these made me aware of the richness and complexity of human language, and laid the foundation for my conviction which developed in seminary that there could be no perfect translation of the Scriptures. It was my three years study of Hebrew that confirmed this conviction. Several of my teachers convinced me of the need to be able, as a minister, to make my own translation. I seldom do this, but my work in language makes it possible at least critically to evaluate the translations I use.

I make occasional use of several translations in study, preaching, and teaching, and I encourage others to do so, but my major attention is confined to two translations. The first is the King James Version which I use in the pulpit generally for three reasons. First,

I still consider it without parallel in terms of its poetic beauty. Second, and closely related, it is traditional, and I like some tradition in public worship. Third, because many still use it, I consider it a good starting point for correcting errors in biblical interpretation which result from archaic or erroneous translations.

The second translation is the *Revised Standard Version,* which I use in personal study and in teaching. My reasons are several. First, I consider its overall accuracy in terms of its fidelity to the ancient languages and manuscripts to be superior to other translations. Second, and closely related, it presents less interpretation than some recent popular versions as, *The Living Bible,* for example, thus leaving the individual free and responsible to come to his own interpretation. Third, no other translation with which I am familiar combines literal accuracy with simple readability quite so well as the *Revised Standard Version.* Finally, I appreciate the way it takes account (in some editions) of various manuscript readings in one margin or footnotes. My favorite edition of this version is *The Oxford Annotated Bible* because its footnotes combine brevity with scholarly excellence without dogmatism in a very helpful way.

Other translations I use occasionally include *The New English Bible, The New Testament in Modern English* by Phillips, and the Moffatt translation.

DR. RALPH H. LANGLEY, pastor, Willow Meadows Baptist Church, Houston, Texas, writes:

For Sunday reading in the pulpit I still count on the King James Version as my favorite. It has a ring of dignity and solemnity and kindles its own reverence. Maybe part of the effect is from tradition and familiarity—maybe even from memorization or a combination of all these values. It has no serious rival for most formal worship settings.

And I have tried Sunday morning sermons with a Scripture

reading from modern versions. Although the effect usually has been disappointing, there have been a few notable exceptions. Last Christmas I used Clarence Jordan's Cotton-Patch version of Luke's Gospel to jolt listeners a little out of the ruts of the overly familiar. Jordan has Jesus being born in Gainesville, Georgia (holy family up from Valdosta!) and the child laid in an apple box. This time I got a different and desired effect. Jordan's down-home-in-Georgia accent on records has also been a desirable jolt for our Wednesday and Thursday Bible studies. A page of Paul's epistles in "Jordanese" is an eye-opener—often a heart-opener! His treatment of the Sermon on the Mount is probing and penetrating stuff. His Macon, Georgia setting of the Good Samaritan has radium burns in it.

Sometimes I start a sermon with the passage in the King James and then read from several other versions to bring out greater insight and accuracy against the backdrop of the old and familiar. The *New English Bible* is one of the best for this purpose. Also I like for this purpose *The New Testament in the Language of the People* by Charles B. Williams (one of the few done by a Baptist scholar). It is especially helpful with verb forms and never fails to add light to a passage as its verbs and tenses come alive under Williams' skill in the syntax of Greek verb-forms.

In our church we have copies of the *Today's English Version* of the New Testament in the pews. In this way we encourage the use of the Scriptures, even if the parishioners have failed to bring their personal Bibles. I urge them to read with their eyes while I read the passage aloud. The point is participation, and the opening of many Bibles is a great gain. The more versions in evidence, the better the chance for enlightenment.

Each translation is of necessity an interpretation. All versions—like all Scriptures—are not of equal value and importance. But translation/or paraphrase/or commentary—they all have the potential of great blessing and inspiration. I keep a number of other Bibles in my study, and often benefit from "comparisons." Curtis Vaughan has rendered a real service with his *New Testament from*

26 Translations, showing distinctive differences. It's ideal for group Bible discussion, especially in giving shades and slants of meaningful insight. We also use *The Four Translation New Testament* with parallel readings to good effect.

A central principle in preaching is to treat the familiar in an unfamiliar way and vice-versa. One of my favorite ways to follow this principle is to use unusual translations that light up the passage. Take Moffatt's version for instance. He is to me very bland in the Psalms. But how he comes alive in a passage like the classic chapter 12 of Ecclesiastes!

I did the same thing with Moffatt's marvelous version of 1 Corinthians 13. I also love the *Centenary Translation of the New Testament* by Helen Barrett Montgomery (happily another Baptist scholar of first rank)—especially her work with the Gospels. I am also quite fond of *The New Testament in Modern English* by J. B. Phillips. His finest hour was his work on Acts, appropriately calling it *The Young Church in Action.*

DR. ROBERT L. LEE, executive secretary-treasurer, Louisiana Baptist Convention, Alexandria, writes:

I read and use the King James Version of the Bible probably because of structure and phraseology so long familiar to the rank and file of English Bible students, including myself.

I do appreciate modern paraphrase faithful to the original text which relates the timeless truth of God's Word in contemporary idiom to make it more understandable in our currently spoken language. I like *The Living Bible, Today's English Version,* Phillips' *The New Testament in Modern English,* and especially *The New English Bible.* In recent years the New Testament in the last named version has become a familiar companion for study, devotional reading, and the pulpit. It is a good translation and makes good reading.

Any one of numerous translations, such as *The New Testament in the Language of the People* by Charles B. Williams, *Revised Standard Version,* or *The Amplified Bible,* complement the King James rendering of given Scripture passages, and I check into one or more when studying a lesson or sermon text. As a former seminary student of the languages, I would like to boast to my esteemed professors that I read the text in Greek and Hebrew, but I must admit that reference to the Scriptures in either of these languages is employed with the help of a lexicon in probing for additional light on the ancient meaning of words or phrases.

Whatever version of the Bible I read, I must know anyway that the abiding and eternal truth therein is revealed to mind and heart by the Holy Spirit.

DR. DAVID O. MOORE, chairman, religion department, William Jewell College, Liberty, Missouri, writes:

The English translation of the Bible I use must accomplish two things: first, accurately represent what was actually said by the writer in the original language, and second, say this in today's spoken English. In other words, it must be a translation and not an interpretation or a paraphrase, and it must be in understandable English.

For my purposes, the *Revised Standard Version* best meets these standards. The King James Version has an aesthetic appeal in its cadence or rhythm and beauty of quaint expression. The RSV catches some of this, but it frees the modern reader from the confusion of words that have changed in meaning, about three hundred of them.

Modern translations use information gained from recent manuscript findings and through archaeological discoveries. These must be fairly and accurately used where there are variant readings in the ancient manuscripts. The RSV has done this, indicating the variants in footnotes. Reading the Preface to the RSV with an open mind can greatly help the Bible student. It will go far toward

clarifying what makes for a good translation as well as how the
Bible must be studied in order for its proper meaning to be clear.

Since no originals of the manuscripts written by biblical men
exist, it is important to arrive at an acceptable text. It would seem
that a more trustworthy conclusion as to the best text could be
reached by a committee of scholars working on the problem of
variant readings than by one person working alone. A community
does not guarantee authenticity, but it does serve as a check and
balance in deciding between possible translations. The RSV meets
this standard of safeguard. Thirty-two scholars made up the translation committee, and they were guided by an advisory board of
fifty persons representing a wide variety of denominations.

One must beware of a translation that is made as a "propaganda"
piece. Such a translator is apt to read through glasses that are
biased toward his point of view. *The Living Bible, a Paraphrase,*
is an illustration of this. The writer, one man, has the biblical
authors stating propositions in his paraphrase that simply are not
in a true translation of those passages. Real danger is inherent
in this since most people accept what is in a printed Bible as "the
Word of God"; therefore for them what is there on the page is
what God actually said through the biblical writers. On this account,
heavy responsibility rests on a translator to present only what was
written by the biblical author.

My own college students want a *study* Bible. This includes:
introductions to each of the books, divisional outlines with titles
printed on the page, copious footnotes to help with difficult passages, adequate margins for personal notations, and concise articles
in an appendix dealing with dates, historical surveys of the biblical
world, a summary of how the Bible came to us through history,
and appropriate maps.

Obviously, we can never have an absolutely perfect Bible translation. Since fallible man must translate, we will always have a human
document recording a divine revelation which was given by God
in history. Whatever translation is acceptable today will not be

so one hundred years from now. Language will change. Surely, new discoveries of other texts will be made. On this account a new translation will have to be made. But certainly for the present the *Revised Standard Version* can serve those who wish seriously to know "the Word of God."

DR. BOB MOWERY, pastor, Park Avenue Baptist Church, Nashville, Tennessee, writes:

More than any other I use *The Amplified Bible* in my personal study. Devotionally, I enjoy *The Living Bible.* From the pulpit I usually read from the King James Version. I have memorized over one hundred chapters of the Bible from the King James Version. During my seminary days, I found the American Standard Version to be most accurate and to be very helpful in my study of the original Hebrew and Greek languages.

DR. FRANKLIN OWEN, executive secretary-treasurer, Kentucky Baptist Convention, Middletown, Kentucky, writes:

I have perhaps a dozen or fifteen translations of the Scriptures. The proliferation of translations has now reached the point that it seems that instead of seeking greater accuracy, the newer translations are simply trying to find a different way to say it and feel obligated to make it as different as possible from previous translations. Thus, the question arises from here on: "How accurate are they?"

More and more, I've been going back to the King James Version, trying to keep in mind the points of inaccuracy and spurious references and using other translations when these are encountered.

No, it is not my age that has led me back to the "King Jim"; I think it is because the modern speech translations lack a reverent way to speak of the Deity. Saying just "you" seems too familiar for me. Whatever else may be said about the "archaic" King James

Version, it certainly had a reverent way of referring to the Divine, and I have not been able to give this up. If that is purely because I was schooled in it, then I am glad I was so schooled.

DR. R. J. ROBINSON, pastor, First Baptist Church, Augusta, Georgia, writes:

My congregation knows that I always read the Scripture publicly from the King James Version—unless I declare otherwise. Sometimes I will insert a short phrase or sentence from another translation.

I study from all available translations (not paraphrases) and the Greek New Testament, and I make much use of *The New Testament from 26 Translations.*

Of course, I employ Robertson's *Harmony of the Gospels* a great deal.

DR. LEONARD SANDERSON, evangelism director, Louisiana Baptist Convention, Alexandria, writes:

The *Revised Standard Version* is my preference as a study and pulpit Bible. The primary reasons are its reliability in translation and its acceptability in public reading.

My second preference is *Today's English Version.* I use it in Lay Evangelism Schools and in witnessing. It is recognized as a good translation, is popular, and can be distributed conveniently to a large group. Most non-Christians today are not familiar with any translation but seem to respond better to a modern translation. In my study I use TEV alongside RSV. If a question arises in study of these two, it is usually better to go to a more basic source.

I use *The New Testament in the Language of the People* by Charles B. Williams for verb translations and for sentimental reasons—he was my old teacher.

The *New English Bible* would be perhaps as acceptable as RSV except for several purely British words used in translation. I use it and *The New Testament in Modern English* by Phillips some in my study. On occasion I quote from Phillips for clarification and variety.

I perhaps memorized more passages in the American Standard Version (1901) than any other translation because I used it during the first ten years of Bible study including college and seminary. I often use the copy given me at my ordination.

For some years I used the King James Version for the convenience of a loose-leaf edition. During such times I tried to keep another translation handy.

On occasion I have used Montgomery, Beck, Moffatt, Barclay, and translations of individual passages by many teachers and scholars. I relish the new translations as they continue to flourish. I enjoy the *Living Bible, Paraphrased* for occasional devotional study.

DR. BILLY E. SIMMONS, chairman, religion department, East Texas Baptist College, Marshall, Texas, writes:

As far as an Old Testament translation is concerned, I prefer the American Standard Version of 1901 above all others at the present time. Though it may be stilted in its language at times, it is still a very faithful translation. It followed the best texts available at the time, and I am persuaded that it is still the best available Old Testament text.

In the New Testament, I prefer the *New American Standard Bible* over all of the major translations available for classroom purposes. I believe that it preserves most faithfully the different kinds of action inherent in the various Greek tenses. It also follows the earliest and best of the Greek manuscripts in its text. Beyond this, the translators have preserved a good literary quality of English. This makes for easy reading but does not destroy the dignity which English readers have appreciated through the years.

For my private reading of an English New Testament, I prefer *The New Testament in Modern English* by J. B. Phillips. It is written in a beautiful literary style, and it preserves very faithfully the intent of the original language. I find the New Testament "comes alive" for me through this paraphrase.

DR. WILLIAM W. STEVENS, chairman, division of religion, Mississippi College, Clinton, writes:

During my seminary days the American Standard Version (1901) was in vogue in most colleges and seminaries. Not only did I use it as a student, but I also received a copy of the American Standard Version at my ordination to the ministry. Thus, in classroom study, sermon preparation, personal devotions, and passage memorization I have used this version. Reluctant to "alter my habit," I must admit that tradition played a significant role in determining my use of a particular translation of the Bible.

This is not to say that I do not see where various passages in the American Standard could be improved by substituting words or phrases nearer to the Hebrew or Greek. For instance, the Greek word translated "only begotten" in John 1:18 really means "only" or "unique." When Jerome produced his Latin Vulgate, he equated the Greek word with a Latin word meaning "only begotten." Early English translations which leaned more on the Vulgate than on Greek manuscripts perpetuated that error. Again, in most of the Pauline passages where the term "dispensation" is found in the American Standard Version, the Greek word is better translated "stewardship" or "management." Since the Greek word does not mean "span of time," the dispensationalists reacted violently to the *Revised Standard Version* at first because the key word of their theological system had been eliminated.

Each translation has its advantages and disadvantages, strengths and weaknesses. It is difficult to decide which is "the best." I do believe that the modern paraphrases, however, so popular today, are the least reliable. *The Living Bible* is a good illustration. Such paraphrases fall short of the meanings of John, Paul, and other biblical writers. *The Living Bible* calls Elizabeth Mary's aunt, but the Greek word means "kinswoman." Because Elizabeth was much older than Mary, the author of this paraphrase assumed she was Mary's aunt, but the Greek does not warrant that assumption.

DR. SCOTT L. TATUM, pastor, Broadmoor Baptist Church, Shreveport, Louisiana, writes:

During my seminary days and part of my first pastorate I used the American Standard Version of the Scriptures almost exclusively in my study. But from my second pastorate to the present I have used the King James Version when reading the Scriptures in the pulpit. When I complete the reading of the Scriptures, I often take a moment to point out words or phrases that seem to need a more accurate translation in the light of current usage. Many of our members have expressed appreciation for my using the King James Version with these clarifications.

As a pastor, I am greatly concerned because so many of our people are using many different translations. It is becoming increasingly difficult for a church to worship with real unity in reading the Scriptures aloud. This is unfortunate. It has robbed our church of one of its finest privileges. We do the best we can by reading either responsively or in unison the passages in the hymnbook.

For many years our church has had a splendid program for children to learn how to use their Bibles and to memorize specific texts. The proliferation of versions and translations now makes it increasingly difficult for us to carry on a consistent program of Scripture memorization.

At one of our recent services, I asked members of our congregation to indicate which translation of the Bible they had in their possession. More than half of them had copies of *The Living Bible.* I think this paraphrase has real value if it is used something like a Bible storybook for children, but I have found many inconsistencies and inaccuracies in it. There are far too many insertions of personal opinion not based on the text of the original language.

Some of our Sunday School teachers and other members of our church have shared with me some of their opinions about translations. One of our teachers said, "These new translations seem to make the Word of God too commonplace." Another said, "Some of my class members are coming to believe error because they have seen it in *The Living Bible*. The very name *'Living Bible'* seems to give to some people the idea that it is superior to other Bibles. The implication is that it is alive while some of the other translations may be to some extent dead."

In my sermon preparation, I read from the *Revised Standard Version*, which I believe is one of the better translations when viewed as a whole. It is most helpful to me to begin with it. After reading from the RSV, I study certain words and phrases in the Greek or Hebrew text with the help of critical commentaries. Following that, I read in devotional commentaries and other works that treat the text at hand.

In addition to the Revised Standard Version and the King James Version, the translations I find most helpful are: *The New Testament in Modern English* by J. B. Phillips, *The New Testament—a Translation in the Language of the People* by Charles B. Williams, *The New Testament in Modern English* by Helen Barrett Montgomery, *The Complete Bible—An American Translation* by Smith and Goodspeed, *The Bible—A New Translation* by James Moffatt, and *Today's English Version.* These are listed in the approximate order of my personal preference.

For quick reference I often refer to *The New Testament from 26 Translations* edited by Curtis Vaughan.

DR. LUTHER JOE THOMPSON, pastor, First Baptist Church, Richmond, Virginia, writes:

The Bible, in whatever manner you may approach it, is the most remarkable book in the world. It is unique in its present and past circulation, in the extent of its translation, and most of all in its effect upon human life.

While the gospel is final and eternal, language is not. Since all language is living and changing the gospel must continually be translated into the idiom of the age. This entails the necessity of continual translation.

Across the years I have used numerous translations and have found most of them profitable. For public reading most frequently I have used the King James Version, believing it easier to correct errors and explain antiquated terms than to forsake the familiarity of memorized texts and the literary beauty of the 1611 translation. Among the more recent versions which I have used in public worship most frequently are *The Bible: A New Translation* by James Moffatt, *The New Testament in Modern English* by J. B. Phillips, and the *New English Bible*—the last being my preference.

The basic accuracy of most of the standard versions is largely dependable, and one's choice is essentially a matter of preference, taste, and purpose. A living Bible presenting a living Lord must continually be put into living language.

DR. JOHN H. TULLOCK, chairman, religion and philosophy department, Belmont College, Nashville, Tennessee, writes:

My basic aim in teaching is to help students learn what the Bible really says because I believe that when they learn this, they will realize that it speaks to their own needs. Most of the students I teach are in survey courses of the Bible, and this is usually the only exposure they have to college level Bible teaching. Thus I have a limited time to accomplish my purposes with them.

For these reasons, the selection of the right version of the Bible to use in teaching and to recommend to students for their reading assignments is doubly important. I use the *Revised Standard Version* because it is written in modern English and is readily available even in inexpensive bindings. Furthermore, it is based upon up-to-date manuscript evidence and thus is more true to the original texts than previous versions. An added advantage is that in recent years at least two fine study editions of the RSV with helpful introductions and notes have been published by Oxford University Press and by Harper and Row.

In New Testament survey courses, I also recommend *Today's English Version,* popularly known as *Good News for Modern Man,* because of its easily understood vocabulary, its outline form, and its wide availability. In upper level Old Testament courses, I prefer *The New English Bible.* Its translation of Hebrew poetry is excellent, more nearly preserving the rhythm of Hebrew poetry in English than any other translation I know. I do not prefer it in upper level New Testament courses because its British idiom may seem strange or even humorous to American ears. I note especially 1 Corinthians 5:9: "I wrote that you must have nothing to do with loose livers." I cannot help but think of hog-killing time in the country when I read this passage because the livers were taken out of the hogs and hung on a limb to keep them away from the dogs. I do not believe that was what Paul meant, however.

I must make special mention of TEV's translation of the book of Job, entitled *Tried and True.* I know of no translation or paraphrase which more clearly brings out the force and mood of the arguments in Job than does this translation. I find the translation of Psalms in TEV equally satisfying. If the work of the TEV translators in the rest of the Old Testament matches these two books, it will be by far the most readable and understandable of all translations.